Mulattoes in the Postbellum South and Beyond

The Invisible Legacy of an Afro-European People, Custom, and Class in America's Binary and Three-Tier Societies

Carlton Dubois McClain

Mulattoes in the Postbellum South and Beyond

The Invisible Legacy of an Afro-European People, Custom, and Class in America's Binary and Three-Tier Societies

Carlton Dubois McClain

CreateSpace Independent Publishing Platform

www.carltonmcclain.com

In dedication to Tresia Marie McClain (née Gantt) and Ruth Ann Yarber (née Levison), my paternal grandmother and maternal great-grandmother, respectively

Preface

This original historiographical book, "Mulattoes in the Postbellum South and Beyond: The Invisible Legacy of an Afro-European People, Custom, and Class in America's Binary and Three-Tier Societies," puts Carlton Dubois McClain's ancestral pedigree into perspective within the context of the historical circumstances relevant to those various unions that occurred between Africans, Europeans, and Native Americans in his lineage. Implementing the knowledge that he came to acquire through his studies, Carlton Dubois McClain builds a historical framework as to the predispositions pitted against historically mixed-race persons and people of color, and he goes on to elaborate on the roots of the socio-economic status of contemporary Americans of black African descent, and how the historically Eurocentric-based power and prejudice of some came to adversely impact both the legacy and current-day condition of an entire community of people. In using his own ancestral family as both a case in point and a solidifier of his argument, Carlton Dubois McClain chronicles, examines, and analyzes the historical place that his mulatto-identified ancestors held in society, and, in the process, he constructs a historically-based premise as to the plight, condition, and legacy of historically mixed-race people in the Postbellum South (or the Southern United States after the American Civil War). In so doing, it is his aspiration that this book brings light to the occurrences pertinent to the historical multi-ethnicity within the United States of America.

Mulattoes in the Postbellum South and Beyond: The l. Legacy of an Afro-European People, Custom, and Cla. America's Binary and Three-Tier Societies
Authored by Carlton Dubois McClain

Contents:

Mulattoes in the Postbellum South and Beyond: The Invisible Legacy of an Afro-European People, Custom, and Class in America's Binary and Three-Tier Societies

Chapter I: "The Racialized Past of Western Culture and its Impact on Colonial and Sovereign America leading into the postbellum era through the Exploitation of Peripheral Peoples and their Exploited Slave Labor"

The concept of race is a multi-layered, multi-faceted complexity that carries a deceptively over-simplified definition to most in this current day and age. Race was conceptualized through time, experience, and through the repeated exploitive oppression of various groups historically. By virtue of those social actions and the agendas of those who ran the world, the concept of race emerged as a socio-political construct that was designed in an effort to bar certain individuals of the rights, privileges, and *modes de vie* that certain groups in particular enjoyed in overwhelmingly disproportionate excesses. These *modes de vie* refer to the level of comfort in regard to goods and services afforded to these particular groups in strict exclusivity. In order to build a general understanding of the social actions and agendas of the powers that were and the powers that continue to be, it is imperative to expose oneself to the defining characteristics of social action and agenda, in addition to the identification of those who manipulated those social actions and agendas in their economic and political favor.

Verily, an action is a purposeful behavior, and such implicit behavior is carried out by an actor. The purpose for which an actor carries out something is an agenda; and the concept of agency is a socio-psychological agenda, and it concerns an estimate of the ability of an individual or a group of persons. Social action regards actions within transactions, which are relationships between specific actors. Social structure acts through those who have agendas, or agents. In a historical context, Western European powers that were on the ascendant way from feudalism to capitalism came to establish control over not only neighboring ethnic groups in Europe, but also other groups from around the world, including various peoples from Africa, Asia, the Americas, and Australasia. In accordance with nineteenth-century economist Karl Marx's (1818-1883) assessment of capitalism in his treatise, "Das Kapital," the capitalist polities of Western Europe came to seize hegemony, dominance, and preeminence in the face of the rest of the world due to the exploitative structural anatomy of the capitalist system as well as the overall capitalist agenda.

In a general sense, the definitive elements of a national economy through a capitalist lens encompass various products that are offered at natural prices generated by the use of competition – supply and demand – and the division of labor. In the capitalist economy, finance, for its input, gets interest, or profit, according to the eighteenth-century Scottish economist, Adam Smith (1723-1790). In this economic system, those who gain the highest profits only do so by the misfortune of those who constitute the labor force. In essence, these working classes, or labor force, are products of exploitation on the mere grounds that they do not receive the income that they are worthy of in accordance to and proportion of the contributions that they make to the wellbeing of the entire system. Therefore, few get rich, others acquire considerable wealth, but most remain in unfavorable conditions. Through the lens of today's society, those who subsist in those unfavorable conditions are generally people who are identified as "black" people, and it is not by mere coincidence that most of these people who are identified as such are by-and-large ravaged by poverty and blight. However, these identifications based on race were initially constructed, as aforementioned, as a meticulously-crafted response to the growing disparage between Europe (particularly the West), and the rest of the world, particularly the Americas, Asia, Australasia, and Africa.

Naturally, people view themselves and their own more favorably than complete strangers based on several factors, namely familiarity as well as embedded social and cultural ideals. Even without the distinction of vast phenotypical differences, many Western Europeans identified Eastern European groups with perceptions that were inconsistent with the noble qualities that they had associated with themselves. As early as the Roman Empire and perhaps even earlier, Slavs and other Eastern-Europe groups were deemed as barbarous, uncultivated, and ruthless, such to the extent that the names that these groups of Eastern Europe self-identified with were conspicuously introduced into the vocabulary of Western European languages as words associated with slander and denunciation. A case in point were the Germanic tribes such as the Vandals, and the associated act of "vandalizing," a concept which derived from the commonplace conventions attributed to this particular group, has a ubiquitously negative connotation associated with it—not only in the English language, but also in several other Germanic and Romance tongues as well.

Similarly, European Jews were historically denounced much in the vein that the aforementioned Germanic tribes were; however, prejudice against those Jews in Europe came to acquire a greater sense of gravity, and, through subsequent systematic measures, such gravity culminated in the European Jewry being given separate racial distinctions altogether, perhaps most infamously and notoriously during the Nazi regime of the Third Reich in the former half of the twentieth century. Throughout European antiquity, Jews were mainly the middle men of society, or shopkeepers, lawyers, doctors, innkeepers, bankers, merchants, skilled workers, and financiers. This was especially the case in Eastern European territories, because capitalism had not fully, or at least not effectively, developed in the states of Eastern Europe. For a large part of European history leading up to the twentieth century, feudalism dominated the various Eastern European states, and the elite class (both magnates and lesser nobility) exercised hegemony over the peasantry. The only people in society that kept things afloat from a widespread socio-economic perspective were the Jews, who constituted a proto-middle class in Eastern European states. Many Jews feared the onslaught of the growing popularity of nationalism, because, with it, the ethnic groups that they once serviced through their shops, offices, and banks, would exercise prejudice over them—so multi-ethnic, multi-national kingdoms like the Austro-Hungarian, Prussian, and Ottoman Empires were polities whose existence the Jewry were more than willing to defend.

Eventually, nationalism won out in the end, and Jews were exposed to rampant prejudice that climaxed during the Nazi regime. In the events leading up to the Third Reich, many Germans were especially embarrassed during this time, because they had endured the famines, hyperinflation, and submissive acquiescence of their mother country in the face of Great Britain and France during the Weimar Republic era. Among the German men, there was a growing sense of wounded masculinity, or a lingering notion that their great losses in previous warfare, namely World War I, had emasculated them of their pride and dignity. The sole resolution to this problem could only be realized through engaging in successive warfare so as to reinforce the noble ideals of Germany that had only existed in the nationalistic mentality of the vengeful German men. They would be vindicated through war; and they would no longer be made a mockery of, because those who were to take the imminent fall would be the Jews; and through popularized Nazi propaganda including the Jewish world conspiracy, the so-called German "Aryan" race would liberate the world that had been, in their zealous estimation, riddled too long by the Jewish Question.

Verily, there were rewards for those individuals who adopted the structuralist nature of Nazism and abandoned their previous affiliations with the local Jewry by taking over those aforementioned lots that the Jews once filled in society. Structuralism was a crucial facet of the Nazi regime, both for the powerful and the power-hungry. Upward social mobility could only be achieved through proving one's allegiance to the Nazi agenda, and those involved were constantly striving to gain favor in the fascist system by competing amongst one another for the favor of a superior. In his book, "East Central Europe in the Modern World: The Small States of the Borderlands from Pre- to Postcommunism," American-based political scientist, Andrew Janos (born 1934) provides an analytical framework to the delayed and retarded modernization process of East-Central Europe. In constructing this framework, Janos cites the advent of fascist Germany and its concurrent Aryanization process as an intentional denigration of the once-vibrant Jewish presence in East-Central European society. On the account of the Jewish world conspiracy that had come to the fore during the height of Nazism, Jews were a distinctive, separate race of people that were inferior to "Aryans" or pure-blooded European groups (Janos 186). Prototypical Aryan characteristics were blonde hair, blue eyes, and keen facial features. These phenotypical ideals were deemed as the most desirable, but the majority of those who were classified within the Aryan race did not, ironically enough, possess most or all of these traits. Within the historical lens of Nazism, this was a particular social construct of "race" that had been invented by prejudice, coupled with the Nazis' acquisition of power.

This social construct of "race" that the Nazis created is by-and-large akin to the social construct of "race" that the Western European powers created upon their contact and eventual dominion over groups of Africa, Asia, Australasia, and the Americas beginning in the fifteenth century. Heavily influenced by Eurocentric standards and ideals, the designation, "mulatto," was an inference of selective groups of people to fabricated scientific notions whose purpose was to, through contemptuous presumptions, hold other groups in humiliating inferiority, and celebrate their own Western European groups in honorific superiority. By their own account, the intermingling of Whites and Blacks was scientifically equivalent to a crossbreeding between horses and donkeys, respectively. Hence, the term, "mulatto," arose during the colonization era of the Americas out of the purport that such multi-ethnic persons were no different than "mules," as the term's Latin etymological origins suggested, for the Whites were noble and fortuitous as horses were, and donkeys, allegedly like Blacks, were stubborn and stout.

Spirituality, namely through biblical accounts that were taken entirely out of context, was used in an effort to rationalize racialized Eurocentric ideals that persisted and endured throughout the colonial era. In definitive terms, Eurocentrism refers to a particular form of ethnocentrism, and it encompasses the notion that Europeans evaluate their own societies as complex and advanced and view others' societies as primitive and less-than. During the era of English settlement of present-day New England, European colonists took to the Bible to validate their conquests of indigenous lands. As twentieth- and twenty-first-century American historian, Howard Zinn (1922-2010) poses in his book "A People's History of the United States," "The Puritans also appealed to the Bible, Psalms 2:8: 'Ask of me, and I shall give thee, the heathen for thine inheritance, and the uttermost parts of the earth for thy possession.'" And to justify their use of force to take the land, they cited Romans 13:2: "Whosoever therefore resisteth the power, resisteth the ordinance of God: and they that resist shall receive to themselves damnation" (Zinn 14). Similarly, in the exploitation and eventual colonization of the African continent, several bourgeois economists made the assertions that the preeminence of Western Europe in the face of less-developed parts of the world was divinely ordained. According to his book, "How Europe Underdeveloped Africa," twentieth-century Guyanese economist, Walter Rodney (1942-1980), assesses that the biblical account of the "hath nots" was used to justify the underdeveloped state of non-Western countries, for those bourgeois economists claimed the twenty-ninth verse of the twenty-fifth chapter of the book of Matthew in substantiating the backwardness of the world outside of Western Europe: "For unto every one that hath shall be given, and he shall have abundance; but from him that hath not shall be taken away even that which he hath" (Rodney 21).

Through time, the concept of race emerged out of white racism; and racism could only be generated out of the disproportionate power that Whites acquired through their exploitation of other peoples, namely colonies, beginning in the fifteenth and sixteenth centuries (Cox). It was only through the coalescence of that said power that Western Whites acquired, coupled with the prejudices that they already had concerning those whom they exploited, that gave way to the emergence of racism, and, subsequently, racial distinctions, codes, delineations, and classifications. These constructed racial designations stemmed only from the differences (some tangible, others intangible) between them and those whom they set out to exploit through colonization, inequitable trade, banditry, warfare, kidnapping, and other trickery. Through the accumulation of capital by exploiting various colonial peripheries throughout the world, white racism eventually succeeded in making the steady accretion toward pervading the world as an integral part of the capitalist mode of production. Initially, white racism existed exclusively as mere prejudice, but through continuously acquired power propelled by colonial exploitation, that powerless, internal prejudice gave way to powerfully external, full-fledged racism that came to pervade the conditions of the status quo as well as mainstream ideals that came to permeate Western culture as a result of Western European advancement in the world.

Although white racism arose out of the coalescence of their acquisition of international power with their unabashedly bigoted prejudices, the political and economic system of slavery did not arise out of that racism, however, but rather out of economic reasons. With that stated, slavery made large contributions to the preconceived notions, theories, and mythical legends about the colonized and enslaved groups from Africa and the Americas. In elaborating on Eurocentric ideologies that were conceived to rationalize the backwardness of African states during Europe's colonial exploitation of the African continent, economist Walter Rodney asserted the following, "It is in line with racist prejudice to say openly or to imply that their countries are more developed because their people are innately superior, and that the responsibility for the economic backwardness of Africa lies in the generic backwardness of the race of black Africans" (Rodney 21).

In the United States of America in particular, the wealth of the nation was, by-and-large, acquired through the backs and labor of enslaved people of black African descent. Slave labor, in essence, contributed to the accumulation of capital in large sums in the Western World from the fifteenth through nineteenth centuries; and, only due to the fact that slavery was too rigid for industrial development, did there arise considerable efforts from Western nations to alter, and, ultimately, abolish the slave system. It is by no coincidence that industrialization first began in Great Britain, which was, consequently, the first nation in the world to not only outlaw the slave trade, but also to abolish slavery altogether. As slavery was created out of economic reasons, it was, similarly, done away with out of economic reasons in turn. The leaders of the United States held little to no affinity for those who they constituted as "black" people, and, acting solely out of the growing industry in the North, particularly in the Middle Atlantic and New England states, the nation's leaders saw little correlation between slavery and the future economic advancement of the country by the middle nineteenth century. As a result, they endeavored to do away with the slave system altogether, much to the dismay of the Southern states and their leaders who had by then grown perhaps too accustomed to the patriarchal hierarchy of the slave system.

As for abolitionism in the North, that specific movement merely, by chance, coincided with Northern elite interests, and, it did not, by any stretch of the imagination, drive it. Much of the population density and major urban centers of the United States were concentrated in the North, largely due to the growing manufacturing and industrial presence there. The South was overwhelmingly agrarian with cities far and few between. The largest urban centers of the time in the South were coastal cities that rose to prominence out of the impetus of the slave trade, among them, Charleston, South Carolina, and Savannah, Georgia. Moreover, the favorableness of the climate in the Southern United States also assisted in its eventual overreliance on slave labor so as to generate a productive economy. A critical reason behind the North's early dismissal of the slave system can be attributed to the fact that it was largely uneconomic to keep slaves throughout the entire year due to the climate of the North which was not too dissimilar to the case in Canada. As so, slavery within the context of playing a pivotal role within the scope of the greater political economy grew increasingly rare, because the harsh winters disallowed large-scale plantation agriculture to develop and flourish as it had in the Southern United States and the Caribbean. These climatic conditions, coupled with the growing industrial presence in the North, prompted all of the New England and Middle Atlantic states to abolish the slavery political system by 1820. Ultimately, the conflict of interests between those in the North and those in the South would eventually lead to the Civil War conflict in the United States during the 1860s.

In this current day and age, the concept of race in the United States of America and abroad is based upon socio-political constructs, and, to a much lesser extent, ancestry, that reflect social and cultural characteristics that are not by any means primarily biological or genetic in reference. But this was not always the case. During American antiquity, the socio-political construct that is race historically relied heavily on ancestry or lineage, because, at the time, that was one of the few defining characteristics that demarcated black from white and white from black. Beginning in the seventeenth century and enduring until the middle nineteenth century, to be black in America was to be a slave, and to be a slave in America was to be black. In order to manipulate the slave system, slaveholders, oftentimes through forceful means, courted with their black slave women, and, in order to multiply upon the system, the progeny of these unions were then classified as slaves. Regardless of phenotype or physical appearance, these scions were given the racial designation of "black," due to the slave condition of their mothers, because, again, negritude implied enslavement. As nineteenth-century African-American orator and abolitionist, Frederick Douglass (1818-1895) asserts in his autobiographical account of "The Narrative of the Life of Frederick Douglass,"

The whisper that my master was my father, may or may not be true; and, true or false, it is of but little consequence to my purpose whilst the fact remains, in all its glaring odiousness, that slaveholders have ordained, and by law established, that the children of slave women shall in all cases follow the condition of their mothers; and this is done too obviously to administer to their own lusts, and make a gratification of their wicked desires profitable as well as pleasurable; for by this cunning arrangement, the slaveholder, in cases not a few, sustains to his slaves the double relation of master and father (Douglass 3).

Throughout the course of his life, Frederick Douglass gradually apprehended the apparently immoral evils of the peculiar institution of slavery. In his slave narrative, Douglass serves as a witness to the acts of terror that slavery entailed as well as the degradation of the bondspersons' will to live through the injustices of the institution of slavery. Through these firsthand experiences as a slave, Douglass acquired a fervent loathing for the practice of slavery in general. As Douglass moved into his adulthood and eventual liberty from the bounds of slavery, he expounded upon his perspectives concerning his opposition to slavery and came to the conclusion that it was both dehumanizing as well as tortuous.

After educating himself, he became a self-made man, and, through his charismatic oratory skills and brilliant mind, he became one of the leading spokespersons in the abolitionist movement, the emancipation of the bondspersons, as well as the full integration of African Americans into American society. By virtue of his initial slave condition, Douglass served as an example of the dehumanization of the slave by the Whites. Moreover, Douglass never became aware of his exact age and birthdate. In fact, he pointed out that slaveholders practiced this tactic in order to keep the slaves thusly ignorant, subordinate, and on par with other livestock and property (Douglass 1). In addition, slave children often gorged from a trough full of coarse cornmeal—rushing when they were called—as if they were pigs scrambling to devour a rare meal (Douglass 27). Therewith, a juvenescent Douglass laid witness to the brutal act of the severe whippings of his Aunt Hester. Her wounds were then grinded in salt so as to foment the gruesomeness of her punishment (Douglass 6). Verily, there was a multitude of injustices and inhumane acts of terror that were committed by Whites in order to suppress the black bondspersons. Douglass thus deemed the institution of slavery in its entirety to be a barbarous evil.

Perhaps nothing convinced Douglass more that bondage was an immoral evil than his own accounts and experiences as a slave—for it was one concept to understand the veritable life of the slave and every implicit wrong that was committed against him; however, it was entirely another to live out the awfulness of it. Douglass lived the life of a slave, and, with it, grasped the veracious meaning of the evil nature of slavery—coercion, belonging to another person, and the essential hopelessness for mobility or change. For considerably too long of a tenure, Douglass, as many slaves, was treated as an animal and was valued alongside the livestock. However, through his fight for freedom, he affirmed his manhood, freedom, and opposition to slavery through believing in change. Through giving an account of his slave life, Douglass convinced the world that slavery was verily an immoral act; and, through his intellectual brilliance, Douglass refuted, repudiated, and debunked the white supremacist notion that slavery was the natural status of Blacks and that they were destined to be eternal laborers. His memoir upheld the amoral nature of slavery and confirmed that Blacks did indeed have the inalienable right to pursue life, liberty, and happiness as equals to Whites in these United States of America.

As previously mentioned, the patriarchal slaveholders of the Antebellum South were willing to go to war with the innovative industrialists of the North in order to protect their dominion and way of life that they had grown accustomed to for generations since colonial times. In the end, however, the industrial North won out, and, successively, there arose radical changes in the structure of the Southern United States ensuing the American Civil War of 1861-1865. There was a plethora of amendments made to the societal, economic, and governmental structures of the Southern United States due to the defeat of their associated Confederate army which, by default, ended the institutional system of slavery in the United States. This period immediately after the American Civil War up until the Compromise of 1877 is historically referred to as the Reconstruction era of the Southern United States, or, in the purpose of this account, the Postbellum South—literally, the Southern United States after the war.

Although Reconstruction yielded revolutionary change, the revolution in itself, even at its culmination, was, at best, partial. This era was titled "Reconstruction" because its objective was to establish a "reconstructed" society that, only through wholesale reparations, would incorporate all peoples involved—regardless of race (Patrick-Wexler 46). However, for reasons related to their ulterior motives, the federal government, which was by-and-large controlled by Northern interests at this time, did not take the necessary steps to ensure the permanency of the revolutionary progress achieved in the Postbellum South. Nonetheless, during this period, there was a drastic increase in federal power and the interpretation, execution, and protection of American law established during this period. Federal government enacted these laws and societal establishments due to the actions of the South leading into and during the Civil War. Those among these actions include the secession of the Southern United

States. In this act, the Southern states withdrew from the Union. The Confederacy, as this coalition of states so named themselves, deemed their actions constitutional by citing the formation of the United States of America as a mere pact or agreement of the colonies to voluntarily form one single body of sovereignty. The South viewed this "Compact Theory" as a voluntary act, with the implication that the South joined the Union by their own volition and that they could similarly depart from the Union by their own volition as well. This implication was upheld by the South Carolina Declaration of Causes of Secession:

> But, to remove all doubt, an amendment was added which declared that the powers not delegated to the United States by the Constitution, nor prohibited by it to the states, are reserved to the states, respectively, or to the people… Thus was established, by compact between the states, a government with defined objects and powers, limited to the express words of the grant (Declaration of the Immediate Causes which Induce and Justify the Secession of South Carolina from the Federal Union).

This radical enactment alone was an underlying revolutionary move that was bound to cause fervor and lead to warfare. During this eventual American Civil War, momentous interests in the Union were simultaneously essaying to make revolutionary change as well. Those among these included those, namely abolitionists, who supported the Emancipation Proclamation—declaring the freedom of all slaves of the Confederate States of America. This virtually came to eventually serve as the preamble to the imminent thirteenth, fourteenth, and fifteenth amendments to the United States Constitution succeeding the antebellum era, or the period of the Southern United States before the Civil War. Respectively, those declarations established the termination of slavery, the exact definition of citizenship of native-born Americans, and the endowment of full rights to freedmen. Because of the wholesale changes made and established during this period, societal structures and relations changed as a result. This change in society was strikingly revolutionary due to the longevity of the societal structures of the antebellum period. Social structure remained stagnant for so long, that many white southerners endeavored to revive it. Known as the "Redeemers," southern white groups such as the Ku Klux Klan, the White League, and the Red Shirts all endeavored to oppress the growing power of black-identified persons, carpetbaggers, and United States troops stationed in the South during and after Reconstruction. These racist, paramilitary groups endeavored to squelch the growing so-called "Black Rule" in the Postbellum South. Those among the many exemplifications of "Black Rule" included black-identified persons holding state and national offices, black-identified persons serving as post masters, as well as black-identified persons acting as sheriffs.

In addition, other social revolutionary changes included land reform, education of black-identified persons, the creation of formal cultural establishments, as well as the access to public places for all. In the Sea Islands of South Carolina and the Mississippi Delta, black-identified persons attained twenty- to forty-acre plots to farm. Furthermore, Southern Republican state governments created the South's first public schools. For the first time, black-identified persons attended schools, and historically-black colleges were established. African Americans could be in public places alongside Whites including in trains and other public means of transit. Moreover, African Americans founded churches and other associational institutions. Although radical progress was made during the Postbellum South, this actuality was by-and-large exacerbated by the fact that the achievements of the Reconstruction era were not longevous or ultimately wholesale. In fact, the legacy of the revolution of Reconstruction was undermined by the fact that it was rather quite partial and temporary. A large part in this was due to white Southern resistance. Like said, the Ku Klux Klan, the White League, the Red Shirts, as well as others all endeavored to subdue the power of black-identified persons, Republicans, scalawags, and even educators of African Americans. They would eventually have their way as they instituted "Black Codes" throughout the South that remained and grew stronger after the Compromise of 1877.

In the end, Northern Whites were only concerned about the economic and financial status of themselves and, to a much lesser extent, the reconciliation of the Union of both the North and the South. In regard to that reconciliation process, many northerners were bitter racists who were more than willing to sacrifice black rights in order to mend the Union back together again. This culminated with the Supreme Court ruling of *United States v. Cruikshank* that ruled that it was up to the specific state to protect the rights of freedmen. With the Southern states falling to Democratic white supremacist rule, the rights of freedmen were radically decimated. Compiled with the federal law of the Amnesty Act, which gave voting rights to former secessionists, white supremacy in the South was almost completely restored. The Compromise of 1877 officially removed all of the Republican troops from the South, which effectively established wholesale Democratic, or white supremacist, rule in the South. This occurrence, by effect, brought about an end to the postbellum era of the South in addition to the advancement made and the advancement still in the act of being formulated there. The paralysis of the active enforcement of the laws established during this era detained any social advancements of America during this time on a large scale especially on the account of persons of color, including black-identified and mulatto-identified persons alike.

To fully grasp the distinction of mulatto-identified people as opposed to those who were black-identified, a differentiation of objective must be established. Whites objectified race when it came to persons of color, and they used various classifications of "race" to bar certain individuals of certain rights, while also allowing limited access to specific rights for others. The identification, "black," was, as aforementioned, based on lineage, particularly matriliny— especially during the slavery era of the United States. The designation, "mulatto," was based not on lineage, but rather on physical appearance—for some who fit the technical definition of the original sense of the word, that is, the first-generational offspring of a white person and a black-identified person, were, in some cases (especially during slavery), identified solely as Blacks, but, in other cases, afforded the privilege for passing as Whites. Phenotype was the key in designating an individual as "mulatto," for a majority of the descendants of black-white mixes fell somewhere in the distinction of possessing appearances that suggested both "white" and "black" ancestry. But some, particularly those who were born to one white parent and one parent that was already of partial white heritage himself or herself, were allotted the opportunity to "pass" as white people, especially if they showed no physical traces of their "black" lineage themselves. Notwithstanding, no matter slave or free in the antebellum era, essentially all of the people who were mulatto-identified were subjected to white racism on the sole account of their blackness. Regardless of the fact that "mulattoes" were purportedly only of partial black African lineage, they faced discrimination, nonetheless, even as a mixed-race people who shared a common European heritage with their fully-white counterparts prior to, during, and succeeding the period of the Postbellum South.

Historically, there were varying degrees of hypodescent that were implemented in the United States in order to classify varying degrees of admixture within a mixed-race person's full ancestral lineage. In the antebellum and postbellum eras of the Southern United States, "mulatto," "colored," "negro," "griffe," "quadroon," "octoroon," and "hexadecaroon" were all hypodescent classifications that were employed in order to classify varying degrees of "blackness." Notwithstanding, no matter which categorization a person of African descent was placed, if he or she showed signs of at least partial African heritage, he or she was, as aforementioned, still discriminated against as a person of a full-black lineage in America. This is in fact why this system of hypodescent was implemented in America—for it ascertained that the white race maintained its superiority by remaining "pure." Thence, anything that was mixed-race, or "tainted" with Negro blood, was inferior and, thusly, not white. This ideological assessment of race notoriously endured throughout the annals of American history and society. The "one-drop rule," as it was so called, ascertained that any knowledgeable trace of African ancestry made a person "black." At its inception, the objective of this rule was that being "black" was such a curse, such a horrible cancer, that if one was tainted with even the slightest drop of this poison, then his or her entire bloodstream was thus infected; thence, no matter what, he or she was contemptuously rendered a "black" person and was subjugated to every bit of oppression that came with it.

As previously introduced, in an effort to bar mixed-race individuals who looked white in appearance from "passing for" those of the white race, the previously-mentioned hypodescent classifications were implemented in order to impede this fateful occurrence from happening. This "fateful occurrence" was labeled "passing" simply because it allowed individuals who had black heritage to identify with and be socially perceived and accepted as a white person. One of the main problems with this system, including the fact that it was accepted as a system, was the fact that many interracial-relationship offspring had a black-identified parent that was already mixed-race, which made the process of defining "mulatto" all the more difficult—because, oftentimes, this black-identified parent was before then mixed-race to some degree, and even the black-identified parent himself or herself did not know if his or her ancestors were previous victims of miscegenation. This was, in part, why "mulatto," which initially meant the offspring of a pure African and a pure European, eventually began to take on a broader meaning—encompassing anyone who had both substantial Negro and Caucasian ancestry. As Floyd James Davis asserts,

> The term "mulatto" was originally used to mean the offspring of a "pure African Negro" and a "pure white." Although the root meaning of mulatto, in Spanish, is "hybrid," "mulatto" came to include the children of unions between Whites and so-called "mixed Negroes." For example, Booker T. Washington and Frederick Douglass, with slave mothers and white fathers, were referred to as mulattoes (Bennett, 1962: 255). To whatever extent their mothers were part white, these men were more than half white. Douglass was evidently part Indian as well, and he looked it (Preston, 1980: 9-10). Washington had reddish hair and gray eyes.

Verily, the terms "black" and "negro" are mutually exclusive in regard to the times in which they were in widespread use. "Negro" was by-and-large replaced by "black" in terms of widespread use in conjunction with the culmination of the "black power" and black civil rights movements culminating in the middle twentieth century. "Black" is a reference to any individual with at least some black African heritage, and "negro," a largely antiquated term that predates the popularity of the usage of "black," is virtually synonymous to "black" in terms of meaning. "African Black" refers to those persons who are of a full black lineage, while both "Negro" and "black" are all-encompassing terms that include both mixed and unmixed African-descended populations alike. As F. James Davis goes on to establish a distinction,

> At the time of the American Revolution, many of the founding fathers had some very light slaves, including some who appeared to be white. The term "colored" seemed for a time to refer only to mulattoes, especially lighter ones, but later it became a euphemism for darker Negroes, even including unmixed blacks. With widespread racial mixture, "Negro" came to mean any slave or descendant of a slave, no matter how much mixed. Eventually in the United States, the terms mulatto, colored, Negro, black, and African American all came to mean people with any known black African ancestry. Mulattoes are racially mixed, to whatever degree, while the terms black, Negro, African American, and colored include both mulattoes and unmixed blacks. As we shall see, these terms have quite different meanings in other countries.

Although there were some minor peculiarities in regard to the racial classifications in regard to the respective colonial powers in Western Europe (the British, French, Spanish, Portuguese, Dutch, etc.), the overarching objective was indeed the same from colony to colony. Due to the fact that civil liberties and duties were directly tied to the amount of white ancestry that an individual possessed, hypodescent categorizations were meticulously stratified, and minute exceptions concerning one's heritage were scrupulously recorded. Although these "race"-based classifications were rigid in regard to definitive, *de jure* characteristics, they were, in *de facto* terms, rooted in impressions based on skin complexion rather than explicit information regarding ancestry.

A "griffe" was an individual who had one "mulatto" parent and one black-identified parent. In other words, this individual had one white grandparent and three "black" grandparents. On the contrary, a "quadroon" was a person that had one African or black-identified grandparent and three grandparents that were classified as white. Both "mulatto" and "quadroon" were designations that constituted part of the race classification used primarily in the Southern United States in the eighteenth and nineteenth centuries. In fact, on the 1890 census, census enumerators were instructed to give the racial designations of "black," "mulatto," "octoroon," or "quadroon," to persons of varying degrees of black African ancestry. Some notable African Americans that fell under the latter distinction prior to, during, and after this period of the South included Sally Hemings (1773-1835), Marie Laveau (1794-1881), Alexander Twilight (1795-1857), Robert Purvis (1810-1898), Hiram Rhodes Revels (1827-1901), brothers Patrick Francis Healy (1830-1910) and James Augustine Healy (1830-1900), Pinckney Benton Stewart Pinchback (1837-1921), Adam Clayton Powell, Sr. (1865-1953), among several others.

Chapter II: "The Day-to-day Lives of, the Momentous Events regarding, and the Historically-Documented Designations Given to the Mulatto-identified Persons Prior to, During, and Succeeding the era of the Postbellum South and Beyond"

The life and livelihood of the mulatto-identified individual varied greatly especially during the antebellum era, but also leading into the postbellum era of the South as well. Some were afforded the privilege of living as free persons of color, or, "Free Negroes," as they were customarily identified in appellation; others, who showed no physical traces of their black African lineage, took the decisive action of "passing" for white persons, all in the sole effort to enjoy the rights, privileges, and *modes de vie* that only Whites could enjoy during the time period. However, the vast majority of mulatto-identified persons were confined to institutional enslavement in the Southern United States during the antebellum era. By virtue of this actuality alone, the highest concentration of mulattoes was centered in the Southern United States for reasons relating to the perpetuation of the slave population and its associated institution. As for those free individuals who decided to "pass," they took a momentous risk; for, if their true "race" was revealed, they faced scrupulous castigation and staunch punishment—in so far as enslavement for some of those concurrently-free individuals in the Southern United States. This deferral contributed to the wide variety of phenotypes that the slave population of the Antebellum South possessed—from completely Nordic features to predominantly black African ones. This spectrum was not necessarily tied to degree of admixture, because there remained the possibility that many interracial-relationship offspring could inherit certain phenotypes that were seemingly inconsistent with those of their parentage at face value.

As for the free persons of color, or "Free Negroes" of the Southern United States, their lives were markedly better than the predominant slave population, but it did not come, however, without several restrictions that were associated with the fact that they were non-white and treated as subordinates to Whites in a white, racist society. Nevertheless, there were parts of the South, most notably Charleston, South Carolina, where Free Negroes were afforded lifestyles that were not substantially beneath the white populace there. In fact, many of those Charleston Free Negroes had accrued so much wealth to the point that they became slave-owning themselves. In French- and Spanish-influenced areas of the South, particularly in present-day Louisiana and the Gulf Coast regions of coastal Mississippi and Alabama, free persons of color, or *gens de couleur libres* as they were called in French, enjoyed considerably favorable rights in likeness to their wholly-European counterparts.

French and Latin America was modeled after Romance-speaking Europe, which had varying degrees of social rank based on the quantifying of European ancestry within the scope of a mixed-race person's entire ancestral lineage. By contrast, the United States, which was modeled after English slave customs, acquired an "all or nothing" type system in regard to how people of color were treated socio-economically. This is, in part, the reason behind French- and Spanish-influenced Louisiana consisting of a three-tier society founded upon degrees of white ancestry, while Anglo-America eventually imposed a binary one based on racial background.

A great deal of those multi-ethnic individuals of French- and Spanish-controlled Louisiana were, to a much greater proportion and extent than Free Negroes in other parts of the South, slaveholders themselves as well, and many set out to continue the institution of slavery, because their families had profited, much like the white southerners, from it for generations. As a result, in an attempt to receive more acceptance from the white population, many free persons of color aspired to maintain slavery in order to distance themselves from their black African roots. Notwithstanding, in French- and Spanish-influenced Louisiana and the Anglo-Saxon-dominated South alike, free persons of color were, nonetheless, subjected to public humiliation throughout the antebellum era and ensuing the postbellum era—ranging from social segregation to having legislated curfews. This was not inconsistent with the status quo of the denigrated Jewry during the regime of fascist Germany in the former half of the twentieth century.

As previously mentioned, the majority of the mulatto-identified populace of the Antebellum South came about through the peculiar institution of slavery; and many mulattoes were, nevertheless, slaves in the Antebellum South. Contrary to popular belief, the mulatto slave was not necessarily better off than the black-identified slave. Unbeknownst to many, qualities that were associated with the "good slave" were not at all consistent with connotations largely attributed to the mulatto. A good black slave was subservient, obedient, and unregrettably witless. On the contrary, mulattoes were viewed as threatening, menacing, and insatiably desperate for knowledge and power. Through the lens of those who ruled the slave patriarchal system, the cunning mulatto was a threat to the continuance of slavery—especially the educated one free from the bounds of enslavement. The benign black slave was kept close, but the hazardous mulatto slave was kept closer. And for this reason, the many mulattoes were kept as house servants in the Antebellum South. These mulattoes were deemed the "children of the plantation." As Mary Chestnut remarked towards the conclusion of the antebellum era of South Carolina and the South in its entirety,

This only I see: like the patriarchs of our old men live all in one house with their wives and their concubines; the Mulattoes one sees in every family exactly resemble the white children—every lady tells you who is the father of all the Mulatto children in every body's household, but those in her own, she seems to think drop from the clouds or pretends so to think…

Consequently, these children were subjugated to slavery by law, and were, as a result, given little to no acknowledgement on any significant basis by their white fathers. However, it was not uncommon for wealthy white planters to provide education for their mixed-race progeny. This was oftentimes commonplace in French- and Spanish-influenced colonial possessions, but also, nevertheless, existed in Anglo-influenced America as well. Previously-mentioned brothers, Patrick Francis Healy (1830-1910) and James Augustine Healy (1830-1900) were both born to a white slaveholder, Michael Morris Healy, and his mulatto slave, Mary Eliza, near Macon, Georgia, and they were subsequently sent to be educated at Quaker Schools in Flushing, New York in their boyhood.

Notwithstanding, not all mixed-race African Americans of the time were descendants of wealthy white plantation owners and/or menial overseers and their African or mixed-race concubines and/or slaves. In fact, most of the free, mixed-race African-American families (mulattoes/mulatresses) of the Antebellum South (most notably in Virginia and North Carolina) were either the immediate offspring or multi-generational descendants of "Free Negro" men and their white servant women. Oftentimes, these "Free Negroes" were already mixed-race themselves. A prominent example of this sort of union is David Carll (1842-1910), a "Free Negro" that married a white woman named Mary Louisa Appleford (1844-1899) as far back as 1862.

In regard to the quotidian, everyday lives of those mulattoes who were confined to domestic servitude, these persons ran, in comparison to field slaves, less grueling, but still tedious tasks, nonetheless. Those among these tasks included cooking, serving meals, carding for horses, milking the cows, sewing simple clothes, caring for the master's infant(s), weaving, carding and spinning wool, doing the marketing, churning the milk, dusting the house, sweeping the yard, arranging the dining room, cutting the shrubbery, as well as a multitude of other tasks. Although to a lesser extent, there were field mulattoes as well. Braxton Jackson (1844-1876), the mulatto great-grandfather of my paternal grandfather, was born into slavery in the middle 1840s in the antebellum era and, ensuing emancipation, served as a farm laborer in the town of Stony Creek, Sussex County, Virginia during the postbellum era of the South.

On an ordinary plantation, the typical field slave had a multitude of tasks to complete. After the invention of the cotton gin, many slaveholding communities had intensified the amount of labor that their slaves were to carry out. The work tasks of the field slaves included grubbing and hoeing the field, picking worms off of plants, building fences, cutting down trees, constructing dikes, pulling fodder, clearing new land, planting rice, sugar, tobacco, cotton, and corn, and harvesting the crop afterward. All of these deeds depended upon the season or crop. Mundanely, many field slaves were forced to work from dawn to dusk. Even after their long, tedious day of labor, slaves then had to care for the livestock, put away tools, and cook their own meals before the horn sounded for curfew in the quarters. Failure to complete these respective tasks by either the domestic servants or the field slaves resulted in horrific whippings. Furthermore, the food and housing that the slaves received were almost never satisfactory. Many slaveholders did not provide adequate quantities for their slaves. This resulted in the slaves barely surviving with such meager diets. In order to augment the nutrition in their diets, the slaves stole food when it was denied to them, trapped animals, and/or fished on rest days. Moreover, slaves lived in crudely-built, one-room log cabins. Usually, a multitude of slaves were crammed in confinement to one single cabin. As a result, disease, sickness, and malady often spread amongst the slaves. Over time, the black-descended slave population built immunities and resistance to the adverse conditions that were pitted against them, and, by making the most of their situational circumstances, they survived.

This was part of the reason why Europeans chose to enslave African peoples, because they deemed them to be uncannily strong and durable. During the early stages of the colonial era, Europeans turned to black slave labor due to the fact that they had exhausted the vast majority of the indigenous population of the Americas through disease, starvation, and overexposure. As twentieth- and twenty-first-century historian, Howard Zinn, iterates in "A People's History of the United States," "What Columbus did to the Arawaks of the Bahamas, Cortés did to the Aztecs of Mexico, Pizarro to the Incas of Peru, and the English settlers of Virginia and Massachusetts to the Powhatans and the Pequots" (Zinn 11). In further elaboration, Zinn asserts, "The Indian population of 10 million that lived north of Mexico when Columbus came would ultimately be reduced to less than a million. Huge numbers of Indians would die from diseases introduced by the Whites" (Zinn 16). In bringing clarification to the reasoning behind transitioning from indigenous to black African labor, Zinn assesses,

> Black slaves were the answer. And it was natural to consider imported Blacks as slaves, even if the institution of slavery would not be regularized and legalized for several decades. Because, by 1619, a million Blacks had already been brought from Africa to South America and the

Caribbean, to the Portuguese and Spanish colonies, to work as slaves... So it would have been strange if those twenty Blacks, forcibly transported to Jamestown, and sold as objects to settlers anxious for a steadfast source of labor, were considered as anything but slaves. [Moreover,] their helplessness made enslavement easier. The Indians were on their own land. The Whites were in their own European culture. The Blacks had been torn from their land and culture, forced into a situation where the heritage of language, dress, custom, family relations, was bit by bit obliterated except for the remnants that Blacks could hold on to by sheer, extraordinary persistence (Zinn 25-26).

These original laborers brought to colonial America worked primarily as indentured servants in early colonial times. These laborers included any person, regardless of race, who worked in servitude under contractual obligations for an arranged duration of time—customarily seven years. After this set period of time or tenure came to an end, they were freed and were accordingly given minimal portions of financial and/or environmental capital (such as money or plots of farmland, respectively). As Diane Patrick-Wexler asserts,

Before slavery became official, a small population of free black men and women already lived in the North American colonies. Many of these were indentured servants who had completed their service and were freed. Following their freedom, some began to accumulate money, property, and servants. Some slaves purchased their freedom with money earned on the side, others were freed by owners who made provisions in their wills (Patrick-Wexler 14-15).

Life for the nineteenth-century black- and mulatto-identified descendants of these initial black slave laborers, or indentured servants, of the seventeenth century changed drastically after the emancipation of the bondspersons in the Southern United States. This was the case for both slave and free persons of black African descent everywhere throughout the South. For in the Postbellum South, a new system of society had to be set in place so that these newly-freed persons could receive proper integration into society. For the temporary existence of all but twelve years (1865-1877), this new system of society would encompass the earnest attempt of black sympathizers to fully incorporate Blacks into everyday life. Whether through intentional or unintentional means, the postbellum era yielded an existential reality of a three-tier society throughout the South. At the pinnacle of the societal ladder was the white propertied populace. Below them, were the persons of color that were free during the antebellum era. Lastly, the most abject group of this three-tier society were the former enslaved persons of black African descent. Mulattoes and black-identified individuals, namely the antebellum free persons of color, who had wealth before the war made further strides during this time that culminated in the election of the first African-American governor of the United States. P. B. S. Pinchback (1837-1921), a politician who was born to a white, slaveholding father and his common-law mulatto wife, came to acquire the gubernatorial office in Louisiana. Although his tenure was brief, Pinchback gave African Americans everywhere hope that they too could hold legislative offices throughout the Southern United States.

During the period of the Postbellum South, African Americans for the first time were, as aforementioned, holding offices in the state legislatures and in abundant numbers and fashions as well. However, this sympathy for black-identified individuals and this African-American state of bliss did not last very long, and, in time, white supremacist rule set new laws in place that barred black-identified persons from voting, holding office, and convening in areas and associations set aside for white people. As a result, a new binary division of society was established ensuing the postbellum era, and that division encompassed the identification of every individual of any black African descent as inferior and second-class. This change in the societal structure was especially a major setback for the *gens de couleur libres* (or free persons of color) of Louisiana, coastal Mississippi and Alabama, as well as the corresponding "Free Negro" populace concentrated in satellite cities like Charleston, South Carolina. This aligned them socially with the poverty-riddled freed persons, who, as aforementioned, were historically enslaved by even those *gens de couleur libres* themselves throughout previous generations.

Historically, the Creoles of color were descended from the original *gens de couleur libres* of colonial Louisiana, and neighboring areas such as coastal Alabama and Mississippi. The *gens de couleur libres* were either the immediate offspring or multi-generational descendants of white Creole men and their African or mixed-race concubines, wives, and/or slaves. These women took these men and were generally not forced. There was a system called "plaçage" that characterizes this historical practice. These white men were chiefly of French and/or Spanish heritage, although later immigration from the Germans, Italians, Irishmen, and Jews contributed to the white Creole population of French and Spanish colonial Louisiana and the subsequent American successor state that came to be assimilated into the Antebellum and Postbellum South therewith. The *gens de couleur libres* of colonial and antebellum Louisiana emerged because of these unions, but were not limited to this admixture of European and African, however—as some contained Native American ancestry as well.

As aforementioned, these *gens de couleur libres* almost always married within their own social class in order to retain their lot in society that they worked diligently to attain for generations. Throughout these generations, the Creoles of color enjoyed access to education and property rights that were denied to some other free persons of color in the Antebellum South. Many Creoles of color became classically-trained musicians in the European sort and tradition, and a great deal of them traveled to Paris, France, in accordance with their common French heritage, and many completed their classical studies there. This was not inconsistent with the upbringing of eighteenth-century Afro-French composer, Chevalier de Saint-George (1745-1799), who was born to an ethnically-Wolof slave mother in the French Caribbean colony of Guadeloupe. He was sent, similar to many Creoles of color in French colonial Louisiana, to France to be educated in both classicisms and liberal arts alike. His white father, who was born to the French aristocratic order, went to great lengths to ensure that his mulatto son was granted with the proper tools, skills, and assets as the continuant heir of his line. Chevalier de Saint-George would go on to become one of the most celebrated classical composers in eighteenth-century Europe, and he soon paralleled the popularity of his white contemporaries like Wolfgang Amadeus Mozart (1756-1791) and Joseph Haydn (1732-1809) in pre-revolutionary France.

However, the life and times of Chevalier de Saint-George did not come without brute racism, and his life ended in tragic and melancholic despair. Because of his African ancestry, Saint-George was denied any semblance of normalcy in regard to how he was socially perceived in France as well as maintaining any sense of normalcy in regard to a romantic life. Despite his astounding achievements and accolades, to many, Saint-George was nothing more than a "nigger," and he was treated by many as so—regardless of his wealth, French ancestry, or social standing. Saint-George's expertise as both a musician and composer landed him the appointment of orchestral director of the Royal Opera of Louis XVI under the benefaction of Queen Marie Antoinette. This promotion was much to the chagrin of famous Parisian singers Sophie Arnould and Rosalie Levasseur who addressed the Queen with a petition stating that, "their honor and delicacy of their conscience made it impossible for them to be subjected to the orders of a mulatto" (www.chevalierdesaintgeorge.com).

Moreover, Saint-George's romantic wellbeing was nothing less than taboo—seeing that, as a man of African descent, any relations with white women (which overwhelmingly comprised the female presence in eighteenth-century France) was condemned outright. There was even an account that Saint-George fathered an infant son with a French noblewoman. Upon speculation that the infant child was Saint-George's, the baby was neglected and starved to death. As Swiss historian, Emil Smidak assesses,

> Because of his color, any lasting union was forbidden for Saint-George, partly because marriage between white and colored people was formally prohibited in France from 1778, and partly because none of the noble families with whom he mixed would have wanted to introduce a mulatto descendant into their family tree.

The plight of the individual of African descent was clearly visible during this time, and, in order to work through white racism, people of color looked to work amongst themselves to improve the overall condition of people of color as a whole. As previously mentioned, most Creoles of color of colonial Louisiana fought assiduously to ensure that there was little or no contact between them and the impoverished slave populace of black African descent in a concerted effort to gain more acceptance from Whites and subsequently acquire a higher status in society. Ensuing the freeing of bondspersons, the binary division set in place by white supremacist rule after the postbellum era eradicated any distinctions between the well-off Creoles of color and the former slave population on the sole premise that they shared a common black African heritage. By the estimation of these white supremacists and Southern Democrats, they were all the same on accord of their blackness, regardless of former endowments, wealth, or ancestry.

With the southern supremacists groups' imposition of binary societal divisions, Creoles of color were looking to change the tides ensuing the postbellum era of the South. In Louisiana's primate city of New Orleans, the persons of color there had endured and witnessed the legal and societal racist dominion that white supremacists came to indoctrinate on other groups. In 1891, redeemers even went so far as to erect a monument in commemoration of what is historically referred to as the Battle of Liberty Place—their successful coup of Reconstructionist governmental presence in the area. This monument has since become notorious and violently controversial in the present day, but even then, such a monument was the culmination of several misfortunes that the persons of color had suffered through after the postbellum era.

Five years later in 1896, the New Orleans *Comité des Citoyens* (French for "Committee of the Citizens"), which mainly comprised of Creoles of color and, to a lesser extent, freed persons of color, had carefully arranged the premise for which the case that would later become *Plessy v. Ferguson* would be drawn forth. Through their meticulous arrangement, Homer Plessy (1862-1925), a well-to-do Creole of color of seven-eighths European ancestry (or octoroon), broke the law with sincerest intentions by seating himself in the exclusively-white section of a Louisiana train car, all in the effort to change the unjust status quo of the mulatto- and black-identified populace in the Southern United States under white supremacy. With the backing of the *Comité des Citoyens* of Greater New Orleans, his case eventually reached the federal level, and would go on to become a historical landmark case pertaining to the plight of persons of color succeeding the postbellum era of the South. Ultimately, the case ended in devastating results—as the United States Supreme Court, acting in supposed jurisprudence, made the decisive action to uphold the constitutionality of state legislation requiring the racial segregation of public facilities under the indoctrinated premise of "separate but equal." With that, these persons of color in the Southern United States felt betrayed by the federal law, because the same national legislative body that had overridden and subdued widespread, obtrusive racism in the Postbellum South had, all of a sudden, turned their backs on any concern for the status of America's black- and mulatto-identified persons after the postbellum era. Consequently, the *Plessy v. Ferguson* case came to serve as the institutionalization of this circumstance.

Verily, it is imperative to come to the understanding that the designation that certain multi-ethnic persons were given, "mulatto," was not at all established in open acknowledgment and celebration of the scope of a mixed-race person's full ancestral lineage. Rather, it was implemented, particularly by the census beginning in the year 1790 in the United States of America, in order to gauge the societal relevance of the Eurocentric scientific estimations made about persons born from unions between Whites and black-identified persons. From 1790 through 1840, the United States census, which was observed and taken decennially, mainly designated those who were "Free Negroes" as "mulatto" in historical documentations and recorded manuscripts. During that initial timeframe, "Free Negro" households of the Antebellum South were designated with the same terms that were used for white households. By this order, the "head-of-household" was the sole name given, while all other members of the family were enumerated simply by age and gender.

Customarily, the racial classifications during the Antebellum South used on historical census documentation were "mulatto," "black," and "colored." It was not out of customary line for the census enumerator to list some individuals as one racial distinction and other members of the same household as another. This was due to the fact that racial designations on historical census data were based solely on the account of phenotype, and, coupled with the bitterly racist intent of some southern census enumerators who would more often than not take advantage of their superior writing and literary skills, they manipulated the system of the census to the disadvantage of these antebellum free persons of color. Other times, persons who were listed as "mulatto" on one census would be listed as "black" or, even more drastically, "white" on other censuses. Again, the perception of the enumerator and his or her intent was key in these racial designations given to persons of color during this time.

During the census years of 1850 and 1860, the census introduced separate "slave" and "free" schedules. "Slave" schedules were created to exclusively document the enslaved Blacks, and "free" schedules listed members of all free households, encompassing with it "Free Negro" households. With the exception of notable instances, the "slave" schedules did not, in actuality, list the names of slaves, and, by default of the non-existence of slavery in the North, the "slave" schedules only subsisted in the respective slave states of the Antebellum South. Unlike the early census years of 1790-1840, the "free" schedules of 1850 and 1860 listed the name, age, race, and gender of not only the "head-of-household," but also every other member of the household in addition to newly-introduced qualifications such as those that married within the past year, enrollment into school, as well as literacy level of those over the age of twenty, among other details.

The United States census of 1870 was the inaugural year in which there was a full-fledged effort to assimilate the former black bondspersons into American society, and this 1870 census constituted the only tabulation process during the proper postbellum era of the South, because, by the next census year in 1880, white Southern Democrats and associated groups had by then restored white supremacy throughout the Southern United States that effectively ended the postbellum era. For the first times in certified history, many former slaves took on the official surname of their former slaveholders, and, in adopting those verbal namesakes—both given names and surnames—that they acknowledged during slavery, they would go on to tread as new citizens of America with the vestigial scars of their slave past. For during the antebellum and postbellum eras, slaves and their descendants customarily took on the last name of their master, and the whole town and plantation(s) therein were named in honor of the slave master. As a result, the majority of present-day African Americans bear surnames that are remnant traces, or vestiges, of slave-names, or names that the slave ancestors of many took on under the forceful scrutiny of their former slaveholders.

In assessing a historical framework of the context by which postbellum persons were racially classified, a correlative consonance of the distinctive terminologies in both antiquity and modernity must be assessed in order to acquire a sense of the true meanings of historical racial classifications. The terminology "African American" was introduced in relatively recent times, namely the latter part of the twentieth century. In building a concurrent construct, it is imperative to understand that African Americans are not a mono-racially black "race" group, but are, rather, a largely multiracially-mixed ethnic group. This is due to the fact that there is a common culture, common language, and various racial backgrounds that make up the African-American people today. In defining the true significance of this contemporary ethnic group, it has been widely established, with the benefaction of Harvard University historian, Henry Louis Gates, Jr. (born 1950) and modern geneticists alike, that African Americans are the largely mixed-race descendants of the survivors of the chattel slavery system that took place on the continental United States in large-scale prominence during the antebellum era.

Factually-speaking, a large amount of the African-American people is multi-racially, multi-generationally-mixed. More than seventy percent of the people who are born to two African-American parents are actually of a continual, fully-admixed multi-generationally-mixed ancestral pedigree. This multiracial group within African Americans comprise only of those people who are of a family lineage that consists of ancestral bloodlines which both became and continually remained admixed throughout those respective families' many generations. Hence, having a singular ancestor in antiquity who is found somewhere down the line from umpteen generations ago, whilst everyone since comprises solely of a mono-racial pedigree, does not signify that a person is of a multi-generational, multiracially-mixed lineage, or else the majority of humanity would then have to be deemed of being of this particular multiracial sort. As so, the defining characteristic of this multiracial group within African Americans is attributed to and depends exclusively upon the lineage, and not on the superficially outward, desirably exotic phenotypes that many erroneously associate as a requisite with being of a multiracial heritage.

By contrast, the first-generational-mixed are those people who are the immediate offspring of what is considered to be an interracial relationship. And the contemporary term associated with this variety is "biracial," which, by default of its implication, infers that an individual is an immediate interracial-relationship offspring. In relation to "biracial," the historical terminology "mulatto" can be synonymous to, but is not limited to, the meaning of "biracial." In the context of this current day and age, the term "mulatto" is a largely antiquated pejorative. Notwithstanding, the terminology is appropriate, however, in situations where the term is deemed crucial to the historical context by which it is brought about. Contrary to popular belief, "mulatto" is not a mutually-exclusive synonym to "biracial." In actuality, "mulatto" can be, but is not necessarily, synonymous to "biracial," and the term "mulatto" is also capable of including other groups, although solely within the historical lens of the times in which the term was deemed appropriate, however. It is key to keep in mind that "mulatto" was historically an inclusive term—capable of including anyone who was of a white-black, Afro-European-descended ancestral pedigree; while "biracial" is an exclusive term in contemporary usage—used only to denote those individuals who are the first-generational descendants of unions between Whites and black-identified persons.

The reasoning behind the fact that "mulatto" is no longer deemed socially acceptable in today's context is rooted in the slave past of the United States. In the white supremacists' effort to constrain all potential posterity of interracial unions to a disadvantaged status in the Postbellum South and beyond, a series of racialized legislation in the early twentieth century, centering on the previously-mentioned "one-drop rule," was instituted to, in essence, keep Blacks back in the American socio-economic ladder. Despite the fact that this legislation—officially called the Racial Integrity Laws of 1924 – 1930—was repealed in effect ensuing the *Loving v. Virginia* case by the climax of the Black Civil Rights Movement of the late 1960s, the originally-classified intent of these laws linger on even to this day. Persons of multiracial heritage are still socially perceived as "black" persons in today's society, regardless of their technical racial makeup on the basis of their lineage, and, the way that they are viewed and often discriminated against in society, coupled with the way they are identified by other minority groups exacerbates the perpetuity of such historically racist legislations, by covert and obtrusive means alike.

Chapter III: "The Supplementation of the Personal Account of the Ancestral Pedigree of Carlton Dubois McClain in Contextual Association with the Condition of the Mulattoes of the Postbellum South"

I, Carlton Dubois McClain, am an African American, and, not unlike the majority of the African-American ethnic group in the  United States, I come from a familial pedigree that comprises a racially diverse, albeit complex, ancestral background— consisting of white, black, and indigenous forebears. Verily, I hail from an ancestral lineage that became mixed-race and continued to remain racially-admixed throughout the many generations of my family line leading up to my very own concurrent generation. Thus, I can properly be classified, through the scope of my entire ancestral lineage, as an African

American who is part of the group referred to as "multi-generational, multiracially-mixed" on the account of my paternal and maternal roots alike. As a result, my siblings and I have inherited a multiracial admixture that emanates from both sides of our familial pedigree. Through my mother, I am ultimately of French, African, Choctaw, Creek, Shawnee, Scottish, and Jewish extraction, and, from my paternal lineage, I am of ultimate Anglo-Scots, African, German, and Cherokee descent. Through careful study and research, I have come to the premise that the admixture within my maternal lineage acquired a uniform admixture that had been present for several generations. On the familial side of my father, however, there arose a multitude of divergent interracial interactions occurring quite variably throughout the many generations of my paternal line, particularly through the line of my father's mother.

In addition to me, my parents—the Reverend Coleman Douglas

McClain, Sr., M.Div., MBA (born September 14, 1955) and Evalin Élaine McClain (née Clariette), M.S., MPA (born December 7, 1957), reared two children before me. Among this posterity are Coleman Douglas McClain, Jr., S.B. (born May 18, 1986), a 2011 graduate of the University of Florida in Gainesville, and Cherice Darlana McClain (born September 7, 1989), who attended Saint Louis University during the latter part of the first decade of the twenty-first century.

Moreover, my parents, through their daughter—my sister, Cherice and her husband Javon Keeton Greenwade (born January 24, 1989), have two grandchildren, including Alysia Eliana Greenwade (born August 20, 2009) and Levi Coleman Greenwade (born November 7, 2014). I, Carlton Dubois McClain, A.B. (born April 28, 1992), am the youngest of the three children born to Reverend and Mrs. Coleman Douglas McClain, Sr.

Largely due to his maternal ancestry, my father is a multi-generational, multiracially-mixed African American. My father was born in Greensburg, Pennsylvania on September 14, 1955 to Reginald Denny McClain, Sr. and Tresia Marie McClain (née Gantt). After being honorably discharged from the United States Air Force in 1978, my father enrolled into Bellevue College (now Bellevue University) in suburban Omaha, Nebraska, eventually graduating with a Bachelor of Arts degree in Business Administration in 1982. After relocating south to nearby Kansas City, Kansas shortly after welcoming the birth of my eldest sibling Coleman, Jr. in 1986, my father earned a Master's in Divinity from Central Baptist Theological

Seminary in suburban Kansas City in 1989. His education culminated two decades later with a Master's in Business Administration from Rockhurst University in Kansas City, Missouri in 2009.

My father's father, Reginald Denny McClain, Sr., M.A.,

M.Div. (March 29, 1925 – August 11, 2011) was born on the precipice of the Great Depression in the small western Pennsylvania town of Rankin, which was located eight miles south of Pittsburgh. In his early adulthood, my paternal grandfather attended the Pharmacist Mate School of the United States Naval Reserve in Chicago, Illinois as well as the Field Medical School of Military Corps, Base Camp Lejeune in New River, North Carolina prior to serving in the United

States Navy Reserve. During his tenure in the naval reserve, my paternal grandfather's rank was "Pharmacist Mate 3/C," and he later went on to journey through World War II in the Pacific Theater of War with the First Colored Replacement until he was honorably discharged by the war's end in 1945. My paternal grandfather then went on to earn both undergraduate and graduate degrees in Biblical Studies from Baptist Christian College and successively graduated "magna cum laude" from Shaw University Divinity School in Raleigh, North Carolina with a Master of Divinity in 1993. A decade later in 2003, my paternal grandfather published his autobiographical book, "From Pillar to Post." Through his sixty years of ministry, my paternal grandfather led six different churches of the Baptist denomination throughout New York, North Carolina, and Pennsylvania. Near the end of his illustrious life, my paternal grandfather received the honorable "Governor Robert P. Casey" Medal in 2010 for a "lifetime of service" distinction in Pennsylvania.

In regard to my father's paternal ancestry, my father's father, or my paternal grandfather, Reginald Denny McClain, Sr., was of a lineage that was predominantly black African, or mono-racially black to a considerable degree. His only known white ancestor was his maternal great-great-grandfather, Walsh Jackson, a white overseer from Stony Creek, Sussex County, Virginia. My paternal grandfather was born to Zion McClain, Jr. (April 20, 1902 – November 12, 1945) and his wife Lena Marie Jackson (October 7, 1907 – December 2, 1927). In addition to rearing my paternal grandfather, my great-grandfather, Zion McClain, Jr. and my great-grandmother Lena Marie Jackson welcomed their second child, a daughter named Rosalie (deceased August 21, 2001) on August 9, 1927—just months before Lena perished from edema that stemmed from chronic

myocarditis at the tender age of twenty in December of that same year.

As far as my family knows, there was no known European or Native American ancestry through the lineage of my paternal great-grandfather, Zion McClain, Jr. Like his son and grandson after him, Zion, Jr. lived his life as an ordained Baptist minister, and he was also a skilled pianist as well. His father, Zion McClain, Sr. (January 1855 – October 1, 1933), whose surname was often interchangeably spelled "McClane" during this time period, was born into slavery near the small town of Maxton, North Carolina. Zion McClain, Sr., my paternal great-great-grandfather, went on to wed the daughter of

Eliza Adams, a black slave woman. That daughter, Easter Adams (later Easter McCanns-McClain), my paternal great-great-grandmother, was born in 1864 in North Carolina and perished on November 24, 1926 in Ben Hill County, Georgia near the birthplace of her son, my paternal great-grandfather, Zion McClain, Jr.

According to his autobiographical book, "From Pillar to Post," my paternal grandfather, Reginald McClain, Sr. asserted that, in seeking a better life, the immediate family of Zion McClain, Sr. and his wife Easter had relocated from North Carolina to Fitzgerald, Ben Hill County, Georgia where their children were then born and raised (R. McClain 1). There in Fitzgerald, Georgia, fourteen children, including my paternal great-grandfather Zion McClain, Jr., were born to Zion McClain, Sr. and his wife Easter thereafter. As a note of reference, the family name, McClain, was just a vestige, or remnant, of a slave-name, or a name that my family's slave ancestors took on under the forceful scrutiny of their former slaveholders—and, although the surname "McClain" may misguidedly suggest otherwise, there was little, if any, Scotch-Irish background in my lineage through Zion McClane, Sr. However, the presence of the McClains (or McClanes) was non-coincidentally linked to the Scotch-Irish presence in both Maxton, North Carolina and Fitzgerald, Georgia—for those town names themselves also found roots in Scottish and Irish appellative customs. In fact, the town of Maxton, North Carolina is located in Robeson and Scotland counties—a legacy of the Scotch-Irish influence in the area, and, though spelled differently, the family surname of my great-great-grandfather, Zion McClane, Sr., is shared with the 56th Governor of North Carolina—Angus Wilton McLean (1870 – June 21, 1935), who also shares a birthday (April 20) with my paternal great-grandfather, Zion McClane, Jr.

Furthermore, there was, nevertheless, substantial European ancestry through my paternal grandfather, Reginald McClain, Sr., by way of his mother, Lena Marie Jackson. In remarking of his maternal ancestry, my paternal grandfather, Reginald McClain, Sr., expressed the following, "…[On] my mother's side, all I had seen were light skinned" (R. McClain 11). Lena was of at least one-eighth European ancestry, for her maternal grandfather, Braxton Jackson (1844 – April 16, 1876) was a biracial farm laborer in the Postbellum South, and, on the 1870 census, he was listed as "mulatto" on the account of his European heritage that he acquired from his white father, Walsh Jackson, who was also his mother's overseer. Along with his black slave mother, Tabbi Jackson, the biracial Braxton Jackson, my paternal great-great-great-grandfather, withstood slavery for the first two decades of his life near Stony Creek, Sussex County, Virginia, and, on June 12, 1871, he married Henrietta Booth, a young, former black slave, who was born in 1846 in the same place under similar conditions.

According to the 1870 United States census, which was also the only census Braxton Jackson was tabulated under and also for which he was listed a "mulatto," he could neither read nor write, and his condition had not been improved under the emancipation of the slaves that was instituted in order to guarantee his very own freedom. He would serve as tangible proof that white blood did not necessarily translate into education, status, and wealth. Unfortunately, his former slave condition, through which he was born by the legalized requirement to follow the suit of his black slave mother, disabled him in gaining respectable socio-economic traction—for he was one of those fateful "children of the plantation" and his white overseer father, Walsh Jackson, went to great lengths to abandon any obligation to equip his mulatto son, Braxton Jackson—my great-great-great-grandfather, in a racist world.

As a result, Braxton gained work as a sharecropper. The "sharecropping" system was merely an extension of the slave economy. Both economic measures encompassed the insurmountable debt of the disadvantaged individual in face of the owner or slaveholder. Through the "sharecropping" system, impoverished black- or mulatto-identified persons bartered their own human labor to former slaveholders in order to acquire a share gained from the profit of their labor. Former slaveholders would equip these sharecroppers with several amenities—including cabins, clothes, food, livestock, among several other supplements on credit. This "sharecropping" system was explicitly introduced in order to keep the relationship between Whites and Blacks as strictly "owner" to "debtor," respectively. Oftentimes, these sharecroppers subsisted in slave-like conditions not too dissimilar to enslavement itself, because, through their debts that they were swindled into from the accrued interest indebted to the owner, they attained little likelihood for mobility or change—much like the systemic conditions of slavery itself (Patrick-Wexler 46). Despite the slave conditions that Braxton Jackson was born into, he did eventually accumulate enough capital from his sharecropping endeavors to found his own household in Stony Creek, Sussex County, Virginia by the year 1870.

After growing into manhood, Braxton Jackson acquired the title of "head-of-household" by age twenty-six, living with his wife, Henrietta. Together, Braxton and Henrietta Jackson would go on to rear eleven children, and, one of them, Marie Jackson (later Marie Jackson-Akiens) (September 1876 – 1937), my paternal great-great-grandmother, grew up without ever knowing her father who perished months before her birth. However, she eventually did, through her upbringing in South Boston, Halifax County, Virginia, become aware of his fateful admixture through the oral history that her mother, Henrietta, my paternal great-great-great-grandmother, bestowed upon her through storytelling. Marie Jackson eventually settled down with an African-American fellow, William Jackson, Sr., who was born in August of 1879 in Southern Indiana, with whom she bore several children, including Lena Marie Jackson—the mother of my paternal grandfather, Reginald D. McClain, Sr.

As previously mentioned, through my father's maternal lineage, there existed a plethora of divergent interracial interactions that transpired quite variably throughout the many generations of the pedigree of my father's mother. My paternal grandmother, Tresia

Marie McClain (née Gantt) (March 12, 1928 – November 3, 2017) has, since her marriage on February 27, 1947 to my now-deceased paternal grandfather, Reginald Denny McClain, Sr. in Baltimore, Maryland, become an accomplished paintress as well as a diligent and dutiful homemaker, mothering, including my own father, Coleman Douglas McClain, Sr., seven biological children and one adopted daughter with Reginald McClain, Sr., my paternal grandfather. Outside of my father, Tresia and Reginald McClain bore six other children and an additional adopted daughter, among them, Reginald Denny McClain, Jr. (June 3, 1947 – May 24, 1983), who was born blue-eyed and later emigrated, after several Vietnam War stints in the United States Army, to the United Kingdom, where he married an Englishwoman formerly known as Anne Heathcote, and welcomed my elder cousins (including the blue-eyed Laura Catherine

McClain (born February 18, 1982)), who were all weaned in Liverpool, England. The other posterity of the union of my paternal grandparents—Reginald McClain, Sr., and Tresia McClain (née Gantt)—were Lawrence Cornelius McClain (born January 4, 1949), Darlana Louise McClain (born July 2, 1950), Zionette Yvonne McClain (born June 22, 1951), Kevin Pierre McClain (born February 28, 1954), Simeon Carlton McClain (born April 15, 1957), and Carole Glendina McClain (born February 17, 1965). My paternal grandparents have since been blessed to witness the multiplication of their posterity, with twenty-nine grandchildren, forty great-grandchildren, and fifteen great-great-grandchildren as of 2017.

My paternal grandmother, Tresia McClain (née Gantt), was born to an interracial, multi-ethnic union. In turn, be as it may, both of her parents were products of distinct interracial unions themselves. Through her father, Robert Hick Gantt (February 7, 1886 – September 11, 1971), my paternal grandmother was of English, German, and African descent; and by way of her mother, Etta Mae Gantt (née Ford) (December 4, 1891 – October 27, 1981) who possessed no black African ancestry at all, my paternal grandmother was descended also from Germans as well as Cherokee Indians. Consequently, all of the siblings of my paternal grandmother were racially listed as "mulatto" on the 1920 United States census. The absence of the inclusion of my paternal grandmother herself on this census was due to the simple fact that she would not be born until eight years after this census was taken. With the doing away with the racial classification "mulatto" by the 1930 United States census, all persons of any known black ancestry were subsequently classified exclusively as "black" or "negro" by the time my paternal grandmother made her initial appearance on official United States census records in 1930 at the age of two.

Her father, Robert Hick Gantt, who was born on February 7, 1886 on an estate in the town of Gantt, Covington County, Alabama,

was a homesteader and an ordained minister in the African Methodist Episcopal Church of Zion denomination and was active in ministry in Westmoreland County, Pennsylvania during the greater part of the twentieth century. Robert Hick Gantt had been born with, and therewith retained, his naturally-blue eye color. His father, Carolina Gantt (1860-1912), my great-great-grandfather, had been born to

Martha Gantt (1835 – October 25, 1913), a mulatto former slave that was born in South Carolina. The paternity of Carolina Gantt remains in obscurity, and, it is thought, through much warranted speculation, that his father was probably also a mulatto himself.

Notwithstanding, it is through the lineage of Martha Gantt, the paternal mulatto grandmother of Robert Hick Gantt, my paternal great-grandfather, that the family of my father's mother is descended from Peter Gaunt, an English emigrant from Lincolnshire, England who had settled in East Sandwich, Massachusetts in 1630. The surname, "Gantt," was merely the Americanized rendering of the British "Gaunt," and, throughout the census years of the Postbellum South and afterward, the family of Robert Hick Gantt, my paternal great-grandfather, oftentimes adopted the British variant of the "Gantt" surname in official documentation. As the patriarch of the colonial settlement of the Americas on the behalf of the Gaunt family, Peter Gaunt, who was also a skilled craftsman, was a descendant of nobility including, but not limited to, John of Gaunt – 1st Duke of Lancaster, his father, Edward III – King of England and Lord of Ireland, in addition to Gilbert de Gaunt, as well as Gilbert's first cousin once removed—Queen Matilda of Flanders (wife of William the Conqueror – 1st Norman King of England), and, ultimately, Charlemagne as well as Alfred the Great – King of the Anglo-Saxons, from whom all the British royal family of today and all forty-four Presidents of the United States also descend.

It was only after establishing themselves in the "New World," that these English-later-American Gaunts acquired estates throughout the South, most notably in Alabama, South Carolina, Virginia, and Maryland. Perhaps the most prosperous plantation and estate that the family had founded during the antebellum era of the South was in the town of Gantt, Alabama. In time, Robert Hick Gantt's father, Carolina Gantt, a product of the Gaunts' prosperity in the Antebellum

South, married Charlotte Dosier (1856-1894). They reared nine children altogether, one of which was my blue-eyed paternal great-grandfather, Robert Hick Gantt. Charlotte Gantt (née Dosier) was born to Paul Dosier, a black slave, and his mulatto wife, Nancy, both of which were born around 1830 in Butler County, Alabama.

The mother of my paternal grandmother was Etta Mae Gantt (née Ford), a proprietress, haberdasher, and shopkeeper who was born on December 4, 1891 to parents Josephine "Jodie" Ford and Hillary Ford. Born in the year 1866, Josephine Ford was a full-blooded Cherokee Indian woman whose family had been native to Alabama for generations. Hillary Ford was a white man of predominantly German descent who later moved to the Indian country in Muskogee County, Oklahoma—eventually succumbing to his death there in 1948. Due to his apt involvement in frontiersman endeavors, he remained largely absent from United States census historical data for many decades in the former half of the twentieth century. Josephine and Hillary Ford reared one other child after Etta Mae Gantt (née Ford), the mother of my paternal grandmother—for nearly eleven years after Etta's birth, a son was subsequently born,

Hillary Jim Charles Ford (August 11, 1902 – March 12, 1970). Josephine and Hillary Ford were divorced by the dawn of the twentieth century, and Josephine Ford later remarried to a southern fellow whose surname was Duncan. Together, they welcomed

two children—a daughter, Fannie Ford (later Fannie Ford-McQuay) (May 1, 1898 – June 13, 1980) and son, Anzy Ford, who was born in 1903 in Alabama.

Josephine "Jodie" Ford, my paternal great-great-grandmother, earned a living as a midwife, specializing in childbirth. Her occupation brought her through several communities across the state of Alabama, among them, Huntsville, Hamptonville, and Gantt, Alabama. Through her experiences with midwifery, she had come across a local white doctor in Covington County, Alabama. As a result of his race, class, and social status, she found this man suitable for her daughter, Etta, my paternal great-grandmother. However, Etta herself did not wish to go through with any relations with this prospective husband that her mother had thrust upon her. Instead, she had her eyes on a blue-eyed African-American man, Robert Hick Gantt, with whom she would eventually go on to marry and have eleven children with—one of them, my paternal grandmother, Tresia Marie McClain (née Gantt).

My mother, Evalin Élaine McClain (née Clariette) (born

December 7, 1957), is, similar to her husband—my father, a multi-generational, multiracially-mixed

African American. However, in contrast to my father's lineage, my mother's admixture emerged out of unions that occurred several generations back in her lineage, but, remained, however, consistent throughout the many generations of the families of both her mother and her father leading up to my mother's very own concurrent generation. My mother was the only child born to Alonzo Lee Patterson (March 30, 1937 – April 9, 2011) and Mary Lou "Peggy" Yarber (January 27, 1940 – June 19, 1997). Through her ancestrally-Creole father, my mother is of French, Choctaw, and African descent; and by way of her mother, Mary Lou Yarber, my mother is descended also from African Americans as well as American Jews, Creek and Shawnee Native Americans, and Scotsmen. During her young adolescence, my mother legally acquired the Creole surname, "Clariette," (a variant of the French "Clairette") due to her favorable sentiments toward the family that played a considerable part in her upbringing—the Clariette family of Omaha, Nebraska. They were also of Louisiana Creole descent, but had no biological relation to my mother, however.

My mother was born Evalin Élaine Yarber on December 7, 1957 in Omaha, Douglas County, Nebraska. In her young adolescence, her name was, as aforementioned, legally changed to "Clariette" and, finally, my mother acquired my father's surname, McClain, in congruence with her marriage to my father, the Rev. Coleman Douglas McClain, Sr. on October 6, 1979. Seven years thereafter, my parents gave birth to a son—my eldest sibling, Coleman Douglas McClain, Jr. on May 18, 1986 at Methodist Hospital in Omaha, Nebraska. Three months succeeding his birth, my parents relocated southward to Kansas City, Kansas so that my father could attend, as aforementioned, Central Baptist Theological Seminary—where he went on to graduate in 1989 with a Master's in Divinity. That same year, my parents welcomed a daughter—my sister, Cherice Darlana McClain on September 7, 1989 at Research Medical Center in Kansas City, Missouri. I, Carlton Dubois McClain was subsequently born on April 28, 1992 at Menorah Medical Center in Kansas City, Missouri. In addition to rearing three children, my parents have also,

as previously mentioncd, had the fortune of welcoming the birth of their grandchildren, Levi Coleman Greenwade on November 7, 2014, and, earlier, Alysia Eliana Greenwade, on August 20, 2009. Alysia retained her naturally blue eye color, and she and her younger brother were both born to Javon Keeton Greenwade and his wife— my sister, Cherice Darlana McClain in Greater St. Louis, Missouri.

After earning a Bachelor of Science in Communications from the University of Nebraska – Omaha in May of 1980, my mother then followed through with further education—going on to graduate in May of 1982 with a Master of Science in Urban Studies, also from the University of Nebraska – Omaha. Later, my mother earned a Master of Public Administration from the University of Missouri – Kansas City in December of 1999. Since completing her education, my mother has been fortunate to procure positions as an Auditor at the City of Kansas City, Missouri in July of 1999, Assistant City Manager at the City of Overland Park, Kansas in March of 2004, and, subsequently, Assistant City Manager of the City of Abilene, Texas in October of 2007. In addition to her many successes in her professional career, she completed coursework towards a Ph.D. in Public Administration from the University of Missouri – Kansas City, and even served as the Chair of the Strategic Planning Committee for the Alliance for Women and Children in addition to serving as the former President of the American Society for Public Administration. In commendation for a decade of service in local government, my mother was awarded the International City/County Manager Association (ICMA) Award in 2007.

My mother's father, Alonzo Lee Patterson, was born to Creole parents of mixed French, African, and Native American ancestry whose families had been native to Louisiana for centuries. During the middle of the twentieth century, the parents of my maternal grandfather had moved north to Omaha, Nebraska in the midst of the childhood of my maternal grandfather. My mother's father, Alonzo, was one of five children born to L. E. Patterson and Ivy Mae Patterson (née Williams). L. E. was one of eight children born in Winn Parish (Paroisse de Winn), Louisiana to Albert Alford Patterson and Harriet (Hattie) Patterson (née Walker). Albert, my maternal great-great-grandfather (whose middle name was recorded as "Alfred" in some sources), was a Creole of color of French, Choctaw, and African extraction who had been born to a well-to-do French- and Louisiana Creole-speaking family in Vermilion Parish (Paroisse de Vermilion), Louisiana in the year 1888. Shortly after the birth of his son, my great-great-grandfather, Albert, anglicized the original French family name of "Patenaude" to "Patterson" under increased pressures to Americanize in an increasingly Anglo-dominated Louisiana in the early 20th century.

The French surname "Patenaude," from which the name "Patterson" is derived, transliterates as "our father," and ultimately comes from the Latin, "Paternoster," and this name was historically found all throughout French Louisiana (including Québec and the Maritime Provinces in Canada). The name originates in the historical county of Champagne, France, and was initially used as an identifier for the vocation of the original bearer, which was typically religious. The historical county of Champagne was governed by the Counts of Vermandois. It is not certain whether or not the family of my great-great-grandfather, Albert, is descended from Frankish nobility such as the Counts of Vermandois; however, it has been confirmed and documented through descent from antiquity, nonetheless, that my mother is in fact descended from the Counts of Vermandois (including Hugh the Great, his daughter, Lady Alice (or Adelaide), and his son-in-law Hubert (or Herbert), 4th Count of Vermandois), by way of my mother's mother, Mary Lou "Peggy" Yarber, and my maternal great-grandmother, Ruth Ann Yarber (née Levison).

Although the initials of his son, "L. E." officially stood for nothing, my maternal great-great-grandfather, Albert Patterson, intended for his son to inherit the French name "Louis Édouard." However, he was discouraged to give his son this name, because of the increasing repression of French-based Creole culture in Louisiana during this time. Around the period of the birth of my great-grandfather, L. E., the state legislature of Louisiana had made English the sole official language statewide, and made volatile attempts to repress any remnants of French- and Louisiana Creole-speaking communities across the state—including the requisite to teach English exclusively in schools through the state. At any rate, the family of my great-grandfather, did, in many ways, retain their cultural affiliations through the practicing of Catholicism, the use of Creole idioms in the home, and through cuisine and classical music.

After growing into manhood, my maternal great-grandfather, L. E. Patterson, who joined Freemasonry as a youth, also went on to enlist into the United States Army and was honorably discharged in 1945 following the conclusion of World War II. Shortly before entering the military, my great-grandfather, L. E. wed Ivy Mae

 Williams in Winn Parish, Louisiana on September 14, 1942. Ivy Mae Patterson (née Williams), my maternal great-grandmother, was born in 1915 to a mulatto-identified planter, Cleveland Williams, who was born in 1880 in Ruston, Lincoln Parish, Louisiana and his wife Winnie Williams (née Amos) of Bethany, Caddo Parish, Louisiana. My great-great-grandparents, Cleveland and Winnie Williams, later emigrated to Greater New Orleans, Louisiana, where my great-great-grandfather, Cleveland, established a plantation in St. Charles Parish, Louisiana in the early 20th century.

Upon returning from his service in the United States Army in 1945, my maternal great-grandfather, L. E. Patterson, began to experience tense racial animosity from Anglo-Americans within the community in rural northwest Louisiana. This hostility from Whites culminated in L. E. having to flee Louisiana in fear of his family's safety when terror from the local Ku Klux Klan chapter reached an unbearable breaking point. According to University of Nebraska –

Omaha alumnus and my grand-uncle, James Patterson, A.B. (the son of L. E. and the younger brother of my late maternal grandfather, Alonzo Lee Patterson), the sons of L. E. were not accustomed to acquiesce to the Anglo-Americans' alleged expectations of etiquette. When a white shopkeeper confronted my great-grandfather, L. E., with the notion that his sons did not address the white storekeepers with "Yes, sir and no, sir," L. E. wittingly responded to the white storeowner by proudly stating, "My sons do not even address me with such etiquette customs; so, why in the world would they even feel the slightest necessity to do so with you?!"

Ensuing L. E.'s altercation with the white storeowner, Anglo-American terror began to be inflicted upon L. E. and his family there in rural northwest Louisiana in the middle-to-late 1940s. This Klansmen terror, which included firebombs on L. E.'s home and, later, a fiery cross being thrown on L. E.'s property, eventually culminated in L. E. uprooting he and his family from Louisiana in the year 1947. However, L. E. could not allow the Anglo-Americans to become aware of his exact whereabouts. Therefore, L. E. initially fled town alone and settled with some relatives in Houston, Texas, earning income as a construction worker before being contacted via postal letters from a brother, Alfred, who lived in Omaha, Nebraska. Meanwhile, my maternal great-grandmother, Ivy Mae Patterson, supported the young family as a farm laborer until being notified that her husband, L. E. had settled in with her brother-in-law, Alfred, in Omaha, Nebraska.

When it was eventually secure enough to do so, Ivy Mae moved her five young children (including my late maternal grandfather, Alonzo Lee Patterson, and my grand-uncle, James Patterson, A.B.), to Omaha, where she was reunited with her husband—my maternal great-grandfather—L. E., in 1949, and there, the family settled and henceforth continued to reside. Though born in Louisiana, my grandfather, Alonzo, spent his formative years in Omaha, where he met and fell in love with a woman by the name of Mary Lou "Peggy" Yarber; though they never married, they eventually welcomed a daughter—my mother, Mrs. Evalin Élaine McClain (née Clariette), M.S., MPA, there in Omaha, Nebraska, in the year 1957.

Both of my great-great-grandparents, Albert Alford Patenaude and his wife Hattie, were ultimately of French, Choctaw, and African extraction. Furthermore, through both sides of his family, Albert Alford Patenaude was descended from French colonial settlers who had established themselves in Louisiana as far back as 1710. Moreover, the Native American ancestry of my great-great-grandfather, Albert Alford Patenaude, traces as far back as eighteenth-century Choctaw Native Americans in central Louisiana. In regard to the partial African ancestry of Albert Alford Patenaude, that heritage most likely originated from various ethnic groups of present-day Senegal who were transported to French colonial possessions including Louisiana territory during what is referred to as the "middle passage." A notorious deportation locale for this ominous journey of the slave trade was the widely-known "Gorée Island" off of the western coast of Senegal. Many African bondspersons originated from the same regions of this western coast of Africa, thus concentrating their cultural affiliations and procuring the preservation of their linguistic and customary orientations. This played a crucial role in the development of the Creole patois in Louisiana—for it was spoken by these imported Africans and it incorporated many features of their own tongues in Africa that contributed to the melting pot of tongues that also included Spanish, French, as well as some Native American languages in Louisiana. The resulting factor in all of this was the Creole variant spoken by French and Spanish colonials, free people of color, and black bondspersons alike.

Many Creole families spoke either Creole or French in their homes, including the parents of L. E. Patterson's father, Albert Alford Patenaude. In order to build both social and political capital in their respective communities, many Creoles of color felt obligated to acclimate themselves to the changing of the times by abandoning their linguistic customs that had been ever-present in their families for generations. In order to succeed in an increasing Anglo-dominated society, Louisiana Creoles, including the family of my maternal great-grandfather, L. E. Patterson, would learn and teach their posterity English exclusively. However, other facets of Creole culture did remain throughout the generations, including the practicing of Catholicism, customary cuisine and affinity of classical and jazz music, as well as historical namesakes and idiomatic phrases. In tribute to this, my French middle name, Dubois, emanates from my mother's celebratory homage to her Creole roots. My middle name, Dubois, which literally means "wooded" in French, is a celebratory tribute to the sylvan terrain of Kisatchie National Forest near the birthplace of my mother's father and our family's Louisiana Creole heritage. In addition, my middle name, Dubois, coincides with the surname of gilded African-American scholar, William Edward Burghardt Du Bois (1868-1963), a Harvard University graduate of mixed French Huguenot, Dutch, English, and African ancestry, and who was also the first African American to earn a doctorate and who formulated the terminology, "Talented Tenth," which also comprised many of my ancestors.

In regard to my given name, my parents decided to name me in honor of the middle name of my youngest paternal uncle, whose date of birth (15 April) is also the Julian Calendar equivalent of my Gregorian Calendar birthday (28 April), and whose name was, in turn, a "reflection of close ties with a spiritual brother, Carlton Jones of Pittsburgh, Pennsylvania." Moreover, my given name, through its

Old English etymological origins, transliterates as, "settlement of free men," which my parents intended to pay homage to communities near my place of birth—namely, Independence and Liberty, Missouri. Those municipalities are, in turn, an allusion to President Andrew Jackson's "independence of character," whose namesake is also the county of my birth. Furthermore, the meaning of my given name, "settlement of free men," coincides with the City of Freetown, Sierra Leone, which is also paired as a sister city with the municipality of my birth—Kansas City, Missouri. Additionally, the date of my birth (28 April) is also the birthday of President James Monroe, whose municipal namesake—Monrovia—is the capital and primate city of the West African nation of Liberia, a country whose name bears a similar meaning to the etymology of my given name— "land of the free." Both Monrovia, Liberia and Freetown, Sierra

Leone constitute the first two permanent African-American settlements on continental Africa.

My mother's mother, Mary Lou Yarber, was born on January 27, 1940 in Omaha, Douglas County, Nebraska to Charles Mack Yarber and Ruth Ann Levison. Charles Mack Yarber, who was mulatto-identified prior to the Racial Integrity Laws of 1924 – 1930, was born in 1920 in Wewoka, Seminole County, Oklahoma to an African-American planter George Yarber, Sr., who was himself born in 1894 in New Boston, Texas, and his mulatress wife, Lillie Yarber (née Gleason), who was born in 1896 in

Ashdown, Arkansas; while, Ruth Levison had been born in 1921 to Black Jews—for both of her parents, Simon Curtis Levison and Eva

Levison were of African-American and Jewish extraction. Furthermore, Simon Levison, who was born on July 23, 1880, also had some Native American ancestry—for his indigenous roots trace all the way back to William H. McIntosh, an illustrious Creek-Scots Chief who was born in 1775 in the Kasihta tribe near present-day Columbus, Georgia. The current County of McIntosh, Oklahoma was named in honor of the Creek-Scots Chief, William H. McIntosh (which is near both the 1948 resting place of my previously-mentioned European-American paternal great-great-grandfather, Hillary Ford (Muskogee County, Oklahoma) as well as close by the 1920 birthplace of my mulatto-identified maternal great-grandfather, Charles Yarber (Seminole County, Oklahoma)). The

area in which Charles Yarber was born was also the birthplace of another prominent Creek Chief, George Washington Grayson (May 12, 1843 – December 2, 1940), who was, similar to my great-grandmother, Ruth Ann Levison, related to the wealthy Scots fur trader Robert Grierson and his high-status Shawnee wife, Sinnugee. In the 1790s, Creek

Chief William H. McIntosh betrothed Elizabeth "Eliza" Grierson (1780 – 1856) (daughter of Robert Grierson and Sinnugee), and

together, the married couple welcomed Chillicothe "Chilly" McIntosh (1795 –1879); who was directly descended from David I – King of the Scots in addition to being the first cousin once removed of the 32nd Governor of Georgia and Princeton University graduate, George McIntosh Troup (1780 – 1856), as well as the great-grandfather of the wife of the father of the sister-in-law of my maternal great-grandmother, Ruth Ann Levison, whose parents, Simon and Eva Levison, were, on account of their lineage and their appearances, both mulatto-identified prior to the 1930 United States census. The census year 1900 was the only exception to their mixed-race designation, as the United States census discarded this racial classification that year, only to re-introduce it for the next two censuses, before doing away with it altogether by the census year 1930. Moreover, by way of my great-grandmother Ruth Ann Levison, I am a direct descendant of not only David I – King of the Scots, but also several other high-ranking European magnates, including, but not limited to, Henry I – King of France, Yaroslav the Wise – Grand Prince of Kievan Rus', and William the Conqueror – 1st Norman King of England.

Both of the families of Simon and Eva Levison originated from Yazoo County, Mississippi. Simon Levison, who was welcomed into this world in 1880, was one of seven children born to Muska Levison (born 1850) and Louisa Levison (born 1856) in Yazoo County, Mississippi. After growing into manhood, Simon Levison acquired the title of "head-of-household" by the early twentieth century, and lived along with his wife, Eva, in the Mississippi Delta. Together, Simon and Eva Levison reared six children there in Mississippi, later relocating northward, in conjunction with the overall African-American Great Migration movement, to Omaha, Nebraska, where my great-grandmother, Ruth Levison, was raised, and much of the clan went on to join the upper echelon of Omaha's highly astute

African-American professional community as physicians and attorneys.

My mother's maternal grandfather, Charles Mack Yarber, who was listed racially as "mulatto" on the 1920 United States Census, was, as aforementioned, born to George Yarber, Sr., a New Boston, Texas planter and to his Ashdown, Arkansas-born mulatress wife, Lillie Yarber (née Gleason), both of whom were wed on March 19, 1915. Together, George and Lillie Yarber welcomed six other children outside of my maternal great-grandfather, Charles Mack Yarber. Those children were George, Lena, Garfield, Beatrice, Nathaniel, and Edward. The latter two unfortunately perished in infancy. Under the maiden name, Gleason, Charles Mack Yarber's mother, Lillie Gleason, was one of eight children born to Dave Gleason and Susan Gleason (née Haney).

Originally born into slavery, Dave Gleason married three separate women and went on to father twenty-four children, one of them being Lillie Gleason, my maternal great-great-grandmother. Outside of Susan Gleason (née Haney), the other wives of Dave Gleason were Caroline Gleason and Charity Gleason. The children of Dave and Susan Gleason were Lillie (my maternal great-great-grandmother), Esther, John, Pursac, Jean, Roberta, as well as twins, Monroe and Moses. Susan Gleason later remarried to an African-American man named Porter Johnson, and they subsequently welcomed three sons—Donald, Porter, and James.

Chapter IV: "The Residual Effects of the Historically-disadvantaged
Dispositions of Persons of Color on Contemporary African
Americans"

Due to what came to become the status quo in the United States,
white racism came to eventually serve as the prime justification for
the reason behind why things were the way that they indeed were
(and continue to be in the present day). And a justification was
needed in order to substantiate the ongoing socio-economic
inequalities and disparities between Whites and other ethnic and
racial groups, particularly African Americans—who had historically
been the most abject group in the United States. Verily, changes in
the socio-economic and political system in the West shifted in
response to the problems that these individuals needed to solve. As
technology, or societal tools and skills, advanced and
metamorphosed, culture in the Western World changed in turn; while
ceremony, or the continuous constant entailing societal beliefs,
rituals, and worldviews, remained the same. The agents, or those with
agendas who manipulated the social structure, found that slavery was
becoming an antiquated way for solving the issues of western society.
As a result, they endeavored to do away with the slave system
altogether. However, the ceremonial ideals, or the societal beliefs,

rituals, and worldviews, of the Western World regarding black people remained the same.

In essence, technology and ceremony are two sides of the same coin of "culture." Technology is an ever-changing continuum consisting of societal tools and skills that shifts in response to the problems that humanity is faced with. Ceremony is a continuous constant entailing societal beliefs, rituals, and worldviews that persists throughout generations, centuries, and epochs. In regard to those, namely Western Europeans and their descendants, who manipulated the social structure with their respective agendas, black people, in their eyes, were ceremoniously perceived as inhumane, innately inferior, and unscrupulously vile and cancerous. The Eurocentric view of black people was by no coincidence consistent with the defining characteristics of "blackness" itself—evil, wicked, dishonorable, depressing. In contrast, "whiteness," by its definition, was associated with purity, innocence, and virtue.

In regard to the agenda of those who run the world, it is virtually by default and design that persons of black African descent remain, on the whole, in abject and impoverished conditions. Verily, the root of such social engineering can be found in the ceremonious viewpoints regarding black people. By the estimation of Eurocentric notions, it is the natural disposition of the social structure that persons of black African descent occupy the most inferior lots in society. Although the staunchness and brute obtrusiveness of this objective has waned in the last half century in particular, the original intent of such an objective endures. By a Eurocentric standard and perspective, there is absolutely no way that a person of black African descent can overcome such an unfavorable and disadvantaged state. Verily, there is a colloquialism that characterizes this little man against a formidable adversary, and that statement is, "If the opponent cannot be overcome, then it is in one's best interest to join the company of that opponent." By my estimation, the application of such a colloquialism could be a reference to a person of black African descent intermarrying with Europeans throughout the generations in order to eventually become European. And if that posterity has become European through generations of intermarrying with Whites, then he or she will be able to bask in the rights, privileges, and *modes de vie* that are uniquely specific and restricted to those of European descent.

In response to and denial of such persons who had, through generations, intermixed with Europeans from being socially perceived and accepted as a white person, several laws throughout antiquity were instituted including hypodescent classifications, the "one-drop rule," as well as *partus sequitur ventrem.* The latter legal doctrine in particular, whose Latin appellation transliterated into English as, "that which is brought forth follows the womb," held in the British North American colonies, and subsequently the United States of America, that the slave condition of a child was determined by the slave condition of his or her mother. Such a legal doctrine ascertained that the white slaveholder had a volitional voice in the multiplication of his own slave hands. In order to increase the numbers of his slaves, and thus, increase his lot in society, many slaveholders, as previously mentioned, courted with, forcibly or consensually, with their black female slaves. In correspondence with the *partus* legal institution, the offspring of such unions was to follow the mother as a slave—in order to procure the expansion of institutional slavery, while also making the slaveholder's deepest desires profitable as well as pleasurable—for he maintained the dual distinction as master (profitability) and father (pleasurableness)— which was not inconsistent with the patriarchal arrangement of slavery itself.

Furthermore, in the nineteenth century, Johann Blumenbach invented new classifications of lineage based on physical appearance rather than bloodline through the father. This was imposed in order to elevate a certain group of people who belonged to a particular serpentine lineage. Hence, those who obtrusively looked like Blumenbach, but covertly may or may not have held the bloodline of Blumenbach were privileged. And those who obtrusively looked like Ethiopians (or "Black Africans" in this sense), but covertly held the bloodline of Africa were oppressed. However, those who obtrusively look like Ethiopians, and covertly hold their bloodline, will, in future times, be privileged.

Blumenbach's classifications gave way to the various "modern races" of the world—Caucasians, Amerindians, Africans, East Asians, and Southeast Asians/Aborigines/Pacific Islanders. Notwithstanding, during the slavery era of the United States and the British North American colonies, *partus sequitur ventrem* was enacted in order to destroy a seed that was inherited from those who "looked" like what Blumenbach referred to as "Black Africans." This is why slavery was matrilineal, because the seed inherited from those who looked European would continue to be passed down to the point when the "Black African" race would no longer be prevalent in America.

Virtually, the *partus* legal institution was indoctrinated into society first in the British North American colonies and then afterward in the United States of America due to the legal action of a mixed-race woman by the name of Elizabeth Key Grinstead who successfully sued for her freedom on the premise that she had been born to a white Englishman who was also a member of the House of Burgesses. Her white father had arranged for her freedom from indentured servitude, but such a will was not met upon his death due to a successive arrangement made by a subsequent guardian. With the assistance of William Grinstead—a young English lawyer and Elizabeth Key's common-law husband, Elizabeth sued for her freedom in court and won. As a response to such a landmark case, the Virginia House of Burgesses passed the *partus* law in 1662 which overrode previous precedent set forth by English common law holding that the condition of a child was determined by the condition of his or her father. The status of one's posterity was based on patriliny due to the fact that the father headed the marital union in addition to the progeny brought forth from such a union.

Furthermore, this *partus* law also yielded the union between the black indentured servant and the white woman. This sort of union contributed to the "Free Negro" population in the British North American colonies. Because of the free status of the white woman, her mixed-race offspring would also be free in consistency with the *partus* legal doctrine. This is mainly how "Free Negroes" came into existence—most were descended from men of black African descent who were granted manumission after completing their service in indentured servitude, and the free status of these "Free Negroes" was doubly solidified on the grounds that they were also descended from white women who were free based upon their race alone. After the era of indentured servitude ended, and when all persons of black African descent were subjugated to a lifetime of slave status, manumission was granted from time to time for special circumstances such as the death will of the slaveholder, service in wartimes, or other occasions.

Regarding the status quo of Americans of black African descent, prominent figures in the late nineteenth and early twentieth centuries took action in regard to improving the former adverse conditions of persons of black African descent in the United States of America. Those among these figures included Frederick Douglass, in addition to Booker T. Washington (1856-1915) and William Edward

Burghardt Du Bois. In his Atlanta Cottons and International Exposition Speech, Washington urged African Americans to acquiesce to white supremacy, while also working through the system in order to improve their own condition by attaining an education and "playing by the rules." With such an accomodationist stance, Washington largely appealed to Northern and Southern Whites alike who flocked to underwrite and fund his own Tuskegee Institute. In appeasing white social, racial, and political oppression to the chagrin of the African American, Washington introduced the so-called "hand simile." In such a simile, Washington stated that, "In all things purely social we can be as separate as the fingers, yet one as the hand in all things essential to mutual progress."

Du Bois, who referred to Washington's speech as the "Atlanta Compromise," was an opponent of such acquiescence, and he encouraged the American Negro to withstand white supremacy by contesting the inequality of Whites and Blacks through various organizations. One of those successor organizations, the National Association for the Advancement of Colored People (NAACP), was founded in 1909 by Du Bois himself to bring about social justice for African Americans in their attempt to contend against white racism and supremacy in the North and South alike. According to American historian, Cornel West, "The NAACP was defiant in rhetoric; liberal in vision, legalistic in practice, and headed by elements of the black middle class which often influenced the interests of the organization" (West 6). In response to the valiant attempts by Washington and Du Bois, institutional economist, John R. Commons, asserted that social institutions could not overcome the "genetic inferiority" of African Americans. Commons assessed that African Americans could only parallel the standards of European Americans through "crossbreeding." As Commons went on to declare, "Amalgamation is their door to assimilation. Frederick Douglass, Booker Washington, Professor Du Bois are an honor to any race, but they are mulattoes."

Verily, it is in accordance with white racism that the achievements of an individual of a minority race is solely attributed to the sole factor that that individual is of at least partial European heritage—which, in a Eurocentric viewpoint, serves as the enabling justification behind that person's brilliance and exceptional capacities. This is very much so Commons' assessment of the pioneering qualities of the aforementioned African-American men. In other words, his assessment of them is that they are brilliant because they are not really black—and that their exceptional intellectual capabilities can only be attributed to their white ancestry in honorific exclusivity. This is very much in line with standards of beauty in mainstream culture. Again, culture is part of the overarching social structure, and this structure of society is manipulated by people of wholly European descent. As a result, what is deemed beautiful is determined by Eurocentric standards exclusively. In essence, what is portrayed in the media through commercials, billboards, and advertisements serves as a poignant reminder that what is accepted as a mark of beauty is that which is not associated with features aloof to Eurocentric ideals.

For instance, a mirror is a very intriguing device in modern society. It gives a candid interpretation of oneself and his or her outward phenotype. However, it can also scar, hurt, and demean all by doing nothing other than serving its very own purpose—to reflect. Many are not satisfied with their own reflections, so when they are reminded of them, they are hurt. With society's standards of beauty, this can all come together in the most disastrous of fashions. But a mirror can also serve as a reminder of one's necessity to be proud of himself or herself and how he or she physically appears in front of the rest of the world—regardless if such an appearance is inconsistent with model standards of beauty. Truth is only a negative entity if interpreted as so by those who manipulate the status quo. Therefore, the one who stands in face of the mirror is not tainted by the truthfulness of his or her own reflection. Rather, it is those around that individual that set societal standards that can leave that individual and the rest of the masses believing that what is seen in their very own reflections is something undesirable or ugly. Ultimately, it is up to the individual to be confident in how he or she was created so as to curtail society's definitions of what is beautiful and what is not.

Be as it may, it is very much the mark of the current condition of societal standards when tokens for minority races readily attain European features at face value. For instance, the first African-American Miss America, Vanessa L. Williams (born 1963), drew criticism from the African-American community largely due to the fact that she was regarded as "not black enough," especially when taking into account her fair complexion and blue eyes. Williams, of predominantly African and European descent, came from a well-to-do background and stock. She was raised in an exclusive, majority-white community in Long Island, New York to parents Helen Williams (née Tinch) and Milton Williams, Jr., both of whom were African-American educators. Vanessa Williams' great-great-grandfather, William A. Fields, served as a delegate in the Tennessee state legislature during the era of the Postbellum South, while another great-great-grandfather of Vanessa Williams, David Carll, was a pioneering "Free Negro" who served in the Union Army during the American Civil War. As previously mentioned, Carll went on to marry a white woman, Mary Louisa Appleford, in 1862. Together, they welcomed Vanessa Williams' great-grandfather, Frank Carll.

Over time, admixture within the African-American community entailed status due to the fact that those of historic admixture with

Europeans were afforded more privilege and better social standing. This was the case with the family of Vanessa Williams. This was starkly contrasted with those of recent admixture with Whites. As F. James Davis asserts, "When satisfactory evidence of respectable black parents is lacking, being light-skinned implies illegitimacy and having an underclass white parent and is thus a disgrace in the black community."

Be as it may, Vanessa Williams was handpicked to become a forerunner in regard to African-American firsts for a specific and implicit reason. Oftentimes, these model individuals representing minority races in mainstream culture are to be perceived by the masses as the prototype for the success and wellbeing of the particular minority race that he or she represents. As African-American sociologist, Cornel West, states in his pamphlet, "Toward a Socialist Theory of Racism," "Some influential Blacks were permitted limited opportunities to prosper and thereby seen as models of success for the black masses to emulate." However, this prototypical model that the masses are to in turn model themselves after is largely unrealistic because these standards are drastically inconsistent with the commonalities that these minority groups share and that also make these minority groups unique to themselves.

So, the prototypical ideal is not really part of the distinguishing characteristics that is unique to the minority group that the ideal is purportedly supposed to represent. This contradiction serves as a reminder that, as a minority (particularly African Americans), one cannot advance from the subordinate predisposition that they have been innately faced with. And those who happen to rise above such a disadvantaged state are those who are truly exceptional to their race—and such exceptional qualities is something that the masses cannot, by any realistic means, attain, neither in whole nor in part, that is, by the estimation of Eurocentric ideals, standards, and course of thought.

As aforementioned, the social structure designates that people of African descent subsist in the most subordinate lots of society. By custom, the ceremonial aspect of Eurocentric culture holds that it is the natural status of black people to be inferior. As Robert Cherry evinces in "The Culture-of-Poverty Thesis and African Americans,"

> There was a broad consensus within the economics profession that the inferior status of African Americans reflected genetic inferiority. This consensus began with the founders of the American Economics Association, including Richard Ely and its first president, General Amasa Walker. It was supported by association publications, most notably the monographs by Frederick Hoffman and Joseph Tillinghast.

Even though the blatant implementation of such an agenda has become increasingly covert in relatively recent times, the evidence that such an objective survives can be found in the disparities between Blacks and Whites—whether that be through the generally adverse living conditions, the educational underdevelopment, the income inequalities, the lower life expectancy, or the proportion of incarcerated African-American men in relationship to the total African-American populace in contrast with those imprisoned from the white race. According to the NAACP, of the total incarcerated population of 2.3 million, one million of those imprisoned are African-American, and Blacks are incarcerated at almost six times the rate of Whites. Furthermore, it is not by mere coincidence, and it is indeed by intentional default and design that earning disparities exist between Blacks and Whites, and also between females and males within those racial groups. The median net worth of white households is $81,700; while that of black households is overwhelming less at $10,000. And for every dollar that a white male makes, a black male makes seventy-eight cents; whereas, the white female makes the same as the black male, and the black female makes far less at sixty-eight cents for every white-male dollar. As Cornel West exclaims,

> Institutional forms of racism are embedded in American society in both visible and invisible ways. These institutional forms exist not only in remnants of *de jure* job, housing, and educational discrimination and political gerrymandering. They also manifest themselves in a *de facto* labor market segmentation, produced by the exclusion of large numbers of peoples of color from the socio-economic mainstream. (This exclusion results from limited educational opportunities, devastated families, a disproportionate presence in the prison population, and widespread police brutality.)

In regard to the educational underdevelopment of the African-American child, many black children are not exposed to the level of education necessary in order to equip themselves in an ever-growing competitive world. Per the NAACP, public school districts across the United States that comprise mostly of minority students receive approximately $1,000 less per pupil; and 78% of teachers in those aforementioned minority districts teach in subject areas outside of their accredited subject area. Nonetheless, educator Jean Anyon conducted a study on several New Jersey schools whose results revealed an underlying consistency with the disadvantaged state of the African-American individual. In her study, there were four school types—elite, professional, working class, and poor. The elite schools consisted of children whose parents were chief executive officers; the professional schools comprised children whose parents were doctors, lawyers, etc.; the working class schools attained children whose parents held middle management occupations; and the poor schools comprised children whose parents held the lowest level occupational positions. According to Anyon's study, the written curriculum was the same at face value; however, hidden curriculum was different so as to steer the children in a direction that would lead them to reproduce the socio-economic status of their parentage. In the working class and poor schools, following the rules in strict rigidity was markedly important. In the professional schools, creativity and innovation was key; and in the elite schools, there was rebuttal, which was not only allowed, but also encouraged.

The point of Jean Anyon's study was that the children of these various school types were being conditioned to inherit their parents' lot in life. Through the systematic methods of education, students continue to be taught in accordance with the occupations relevant to the respective social standing of their parents. As Cornel West states in his pamphlet, "Toward a Socialist Theory of Racism,"

> In an increasingly technological society, rural and inner city schools for people of color and many working class and poor Whites serve to reproduce the present racial and class stratified structure of society. Children of the poor, who are disproportionately people of color, are tracked into an impoverished educational system and then face unequal opportunities when they enter the labor force (if steady, meaningful employment is even a possibility).

In essence, white power has played an indelible role in the plight of the contemporary condition of African Americans due to the historical Eurocentric prejudice that drove measures of denigration imposed on black Americans by Whites. For instance, many residential restrictions, most notably redlining as well as the racially restricted covenants, were put in place to maintain the non-black presence in residential areas where Whites lived. On the other hand, the nascent ghettos of American cities were vestiges of proof of the abandonment and disregard for quality and standards of living in areas that were once designated for "Negroes only." Over time, the areas that were historically designated for African Americans gradually began to lag further and further behind those areas historically set aside for Whites, and now there is a stark disparity in regard to development across the city due to the city's racially- and socio-economically-divided past. Verily, the current state of the socio-economic, racial, and socio-political inequality in American cities derives from several historical measures including race-based residential segregation that was implemented through civic laws, codes, and doctrines in order to bar certain individuals of specific racial, ethnic, and socio-economic backgrounds from basking in the wealth generated from the political economy. In essence, the political economy concerns the process whereby the fruits of the economy are acquired by those outside of the economic process. Those that comprise that which is part of the current economic process are generally the working class, and such a labor force consists of minority groups for the most part.

As the minority population continued to grow throughout many American cities, particularly the African-American population, the leading planners of many American urban centers sought out ways to skew such growth. One way in particular encompassed the establishment of residential areas of similarity. Residential areas of similarity refer to those areas whose population belongs to similar socio-economic backgrounds. Thus, the process of implementing such residential development leads to homogeneous residential areas, where there is little to no diversity in regard to household income or socio-economic background. African Americans and other minorities constitute the majority of those who represent lower socio-economic backgrounds, so these residential areas of similarity are, in large part, a racially-segregating measure by default and design.

The implementation of residential areas of similarity was an indirect way of racially segregating the American city, and in the process, it created hyper-segregation throughout the city's urban core. Hyper-segregation refers to ghetto neighborhoods that are highly segregated and isolated, clustered close together, spatially concentrated, and located in the center of the city (Massey and Denton). Hyper-segregation adequately describes the side effects of the enactment of race-based segregation throughout a city—it gives way to poorly developed areas where blight, poverty, and crime prevail. African Americans and other minority groups are most likely to reside in areas where concentrated poverty exists. Those areas comprise of impoverished conditions where 30-40% of the total population is below the poverty line, and more than one-quarter of all African Americans live beneath that poverty line. Verily, the stark contrast between where money was vested and where it was not caused many to question where such blatant inequity generated from, and why it is that those adversely impacted by it continue to mainly be minorities and people of color. It is by no coincidence that, according to the Aspen Institute Roundtable, a neighborhood that largely consists of people of color is more likely to be poorer than an all-white neighborhood, and racial minorities are overrepresented in the poorest and most disadvantaged neighborhoods (The Aspen Institute Roundtable 3).

As previously mentioned, it is virtually impossible, by a Eurocentric standard and perspective, that a person of black African descent can overcome such an unfavorable and disadvantaged state that he or she is born into on the account of his or her blackness. Although John R. Commons assessed, as aforementioned, that only through intermixing with Whites could African Americans come out of their innate inferiority, historical institutions put in place by Western Europeans and their descendants explicitly addressed such intermixing as futile—because, in their eyes, no matter how much European blood a mixed-race person possessed, their blackness alone would forever bar them from being regarded as equals alongside Whites. Notwithstanding, although a mixed-race individual could not attain wholesale equality with Whites in a general sense, this individual was, by virtue of their white heritage, afforded much more opportunity than the African Black. In addressing his own experiences with power, prejudice, and discrimination, my paternal grandfather, Reginald D. McClain, Sr. remarked the following, "There was a familiar cliché quoted by Blacks: 'If you are white, you are right; if you are brown, you can stick around; if you are black, get back.'" Such an existential reality was, in essence, the nature of the historical three-tier society dating back to the colonial period of the Americas.

Such an arrangement was not at all inconsistent with the *casta* system of Latin America during colonial times. This system came to the fore to rationalize the social standing of the mixed-race people that emerged during the post-conquest era of colonial Latin America. These people who were brought forth, or created (hence the term *créole* or *criollo*—from Latin *creare* meaning "to create"), had to be put into perspective in regard to their place and lot in society. However, the classification of one's social standing—determined by heritage, race, ethnic origin, and skin tone—went far beyond the bounds of polity, economy, and society. This societal arrangement indeed both drove and determined every aspect pertaining to these individuals in the *casta* system. Verily, there was a strict relationship between one's race and standing in society. The more European ancestry one possessed, the more privilege and capital they were afforded; while ancestry from those groups regarded as inferior (namely indigenous populations or Africans), resulted in subordination, impoverished conditions, and limited access to resources vital to upward social mobility such as education and capital.

From this juncture arose terminology like "mulatto" in Spanish and Portuguese colonial America, and such terminology entered the linguistic realms of fellow European colonial powers including the English, the French, and the Dutch. As previously introduced, this classification, "mulatto," which was propelled by Eurocentric standards and ideals, was an inference of selective groups of people to fabricated scientific notions whose purpose was to, through contemptuous presumptions, hold other groups in humiliating inferiority, and celebrate their own Western European groups in honorific superiority. By their own account, the intermingling of Whites and Blacks was, as aforementioned, scientifically equivalent to a crossbreeding between horses and donkeys, respectively. Hence, the term, "mulatto," arose during the colonization era of the Americas out of the purport that such multi-ethnic persons were equivalent to "mules," as the term's Latin etymological origins suggested, for Blacks, allegedly like donkeys, were stubborn and stout, while the Whites were noble and fortuitous as horses were.

Although the African Black might make valiant attempts to integrate himself into a society that was dominated by those of European descent by intermixing with Whites throughout the generations, he will never attain full assimilation based upon the sole racist notion that the blackness of him and his posterity renders it impossible to gain social standing on par with those of wholly European descent. Such a reality finds evidence in the socio-racial classifications of the African Black throughout generational admixing with Europeans in not only colonial Latin America, but also in British North American colonies and later the United States of America—

especially the South in the antebellum and postbellum eras alike. For instance, in the *casta* system produced by Miguel Cabrera in 1763,

the product of a union between a white Spaniard and an African Black rendered a "mulatto."

A mulatto's offspring with a white Spaniard was regarded as a "morisco." If a "morisco" intermixed with Whites, an "albino" was begotten. In line with racist notions, the fourth generation admixture of those of black African descent with Whites rendered a "torna atrás" (or "look the other way"), which served as a fateful reminder that, no matter how much the African Black mixed with Whites, he and his progeny would never become white themselves, and would never achieve equality with Whites, or the *gente de razón* (rational people) as Whites saw themselves.

The British North American colonies had a similar arrangement in regard to how first, second, third, and successive generations of Blacks intermingling with Whites were socially regarded and perceived. The first generational-mixed were "mulatto." Whereas the second generational-mixed were regarded as "morisco" in colonial Latin America, "quadroon" became the accepted equivalent in British North America and, later, the United States. "Octoroons" were the English equivalent of the Latin term "albino." And the "torna atrás" found its English rendering in the terminology, "hexadecaroon." All of these classifications were legally instituted in order to keep

African Blacks and their posterity back, because, as previously mentioned, it was the innate place for Blacks to be inferior, and nothing that he or she did as a black person would change that Eurocentric mentality.

However, even though the racially-admixed individual could not attain wholesale equality with Whites in a general sense, this individual, as previously mentioned, was, by virtue of their white heritage, afforded much more opportunity than the African Black. The light skin that was acquired from a mixed-race individual's white heritage was something that built social capital, or the economic value in building and sustaining relationships among people through networking and marketing, which, in turn, went on to establish that individual's brand—resulting in the upward mobility of that mixed-race individual's socio-economic status. As opposed to Anglo-controlled North America, race mixing in Latin colonial possessions was much more of a quotidian commonality in everyday society. In French- and Spanish-controlled areas of the modern-day southeastern United States, a meritocracy developed centering on whiteness. In other words, an individual was equipped with status, wealth, and privilege based on the fairness of his or her skin complexion.

The extralegal system of "plaçage" characterizes such a meritocracy. This system impacted colonial Louisiana and neighboring locales such as Mobile, Alabama, St. Augustine and Pensacola, Florida, and Natchez and Biloxi, Mississippi. In this system, white Creole men entered into left-handed marriages with African or mixed-race women who were then known as *placées*. White Creole men entered into these unions initially due to the underwhelming presence of their own women—for the white woman was scarce in the initial stages of the colonial era. Therefore, white men took black, and later, mixed-race women as common-law wives, mistresses, or concubines, or *placées*. Over generations, the mothers of these *placées* arranged for these unions, and, in turn, received dowry, reverent social status, and, in some cases when appropriate, freedom if enslaved. There were social events, most infamously the "quadroon balls," that encouraged both white Creole men and African or mixed-race women to enter into these common-law marriages and/or concubinages.

There was indeed an economic aspect to the mixed-race individual. According to Monique Guillory, light skin was valued as a social determinant in regard to the status of an individual. As Guillory states, "light skin…commanded a higher price on the slave block, where light-skinned girls fetched much higher prices than did prime field hands." This has, unfortunately, not changed—even as technology has advanced throughout the generations, centuries, and epochs. In more ways than not, ceremony persists. Light skin amongst people of color is regarded as a status symbol. This is very much in line with the 1968 study conducted by Ray Rist—who composed a thesis pertaining to reading tables in African-American children's schools. These tables were not at all based on tests, because tests were not given to the children. Instead, it was based on a hierarchy centering on dress, hygiene, and, most notably, skin tone. The first reading table, known as the "tigers," was given the most attention; the second reading table, or the "sparrows," was given moderate attention, and the third reading table, regarded as the "clowns," was given the least attention. The "clowns" comprised, incoincidentally, the darkest-skinned children.

This is very much in accordance with colorism within the African-American community. The "brown paper bag" test was used in order to bar darker-skinned individuals from entering into elite and exclusive social circles that lighter-skinned Blacks formulated. If one's complexion was darker than that of a "brown paper bag," then he or she was not good enough to enter into the upper echelons of social standing and rank. These upper echelons comprised historically-black colleges and universities such as Spelman College in Atlanta, historically-black fraternities and sororities, as well as many widely-known churches and social groups. In addition to the "brown paper bag" test, the "door test," whose purpose was to bar those individuals whose complexion was darker than that of the church door, as well as the "comb test," which was given to deny those individuals whose hair was too coarse to let a comb sift through, were implemented as a means to build solidarity between lighter-skinned individuals and accordingly advance through society through one's proximity to whiteness (Russell-Cole).

Perhaps the most meticulous means of induction into these exclusive circles was the "blue vein" requisite, which welcomed only those whose complexion was light enough so that the blood could be seen flowing through the veins of the individual's wrists. Such notions and systematic procedures is very much a signification of self-loathing—for it continues along the lines of the ceremonious premise of white racism. Instead of celebrating the commonalities that lighter-skinned and darker-skinned Blacks share, they are looking to a white standard to determine what is deemed as socially acceptable and what is not. The social value of light skin in this relatively contemporary circumstance and context is no different than the social value of light skin in the slavery era of the colonial Americas. This is an underlying reasoning behind the backwardness of black people everywhere—Blacks are looking to Whites to determine a standard of what is valuable and what is not—which is the very defining principle of ceremonious Eurocentrism itself. Instead, Blacks should look within themselves and their own to establish a means of moving forward and advancing in a society where they have been given to a disadvantaged start as a people in the first place.

Chapter V: "The Impact of the Mixed-race Legacy of the African-
American People on the Absence of a Present-day Biracial
Community"

Due in large part to historical existentialities in the United States
of America, the African-American ethnic group comprises largely of
mixed-race people of varying degrees of African, European, and, to a
lesser degree, Native American descent. These existentialities include
the fact that, during colonial indentured servitude, Africans and
Europeans lived and worked in close proximity—which, as
aforementioned, yielded unions or even marriages between African
men and European women. These unions, some legal, others
extralegal, served as the precursor to the "Free Negro" families in
seventeenth-, eighteenth-, and nineteenth-century Virginia and North
Carolina. Again, the status of the progeny yielded from these unions
was free because of the fact that these antebellum mulattoes and
mulatresses were descended from white women—which solidified
the free status of these begotten "Free Negroes" based upon the race
of their matriliny alone. After indentured servitude became
antiquated in regard to labor demands, and when all persons of black
African descent were consigned to a lifetime of slave status, most
mulattoes from the early eighteenth century onward were descended
from enslaved black women who, either forcefully or consensually,
were used for sexual purposes by white slaveholders and/or overseers
in order to multiply upon the numbers of the slave property that they
owned. As F. James Davis asserts,

> Rapes occurred, and many slave women were forced to
> submit regularly to white males or suffer harsh
> consequences. However, slave girls often courted a sexual
> relationship with the master, or another male in the family,
> as a way of gaining distinction among the slaves, avoiding

field work, and obtaining special jobs and other favored treatment for their mixed children (Reuter, 1970: 129).

Occasionally and less frequently, there were consensual relationships between persons of different racial groups as was the case with David Carll's 1862 marriage to his white wife, Mary Louisa Appleford. F. James Davis elaborates on this sort of union further as he assesses, "Sexual contacts between the races also included prostitution, adventure, concubinage, and sometimes love. In rare instances, where free Blacks were concerned, there was even marriage" (Bennett, 1962: 243-68).

In addition to unions between Free Negro men and white women, like that of David Carll and Mary Louisa Appleford, there did exist, nevertheless, marriages between white slaveholders and their common-law African-descended wives that these slave owners had freed along with the mixed-race offspring produced from these unions. This was the case with previously-mentioned P. B. S. Pinchback and his parentage as well as with the parents of Joseph Jenkins Roberts. The latter became the first president of Liberia—one of the first African-American colonies on continental Africa—and his mother, Amelia Roberts, was described as a fair-skinned mulatto woman who procured her freedom from a Welsh planter, who was also Joseph Jenkins Roberts' father. After founding the colony of Liberia, the African-American settlers there began to self-identify as "Americo-Liberians," and they exercised control over Liberia for well over a century. Due to their dominion, the subsequent nation of Liberia was long modeled after the societal structures of the Southern United States, and intermarriage between the Americo-Liberians and the natives in Africa was very much a social taboo and was rarely done—which was not too dissimilar to the social customs practiced within the mulatto elite circles of the United States.

According to ethnographic studies by modern geneticists and historians like Henry Louis Gates, Jr., African Americans, in definitive terms, are a largely multiracially-mixed ethnic group that are the direct descendants of the survivors of the chattel slavery system that once existed in the continental United States. Gates even went on to conclusively state the following in 2009:

> Here are the facts: only 5 percent of African Americans have at least 12.5 percent Native American ancestry, the equivalent of at least one great-grandparent. Those "high cheek bones" and "long, straight black hair" your relatives brag about at every family reunion and holiday meal since you were two years old? Where did they come from? To paraphrase a well-known French saying, 'Seek the white man.'

Verily, present-day African Americans possess certain extents of admixture with white ancestry largely because of a centuries-old presence in the contiguous United States, phenomena pertaining to close proximity with Whites, as well as migration movements within North America. With the help of genetic, genealogical specialists, Harvard University historian, Henry Louis Gates, Jr., discovered the following statistics regarding admixture within African Americans:

- 58 percent of African Americans have at least 12.5% European ancestry (equivalent of one great-grandparent)
- 19.6 percent of African Americans have at least 25% European ancestry (equivalent of one grandparent)
- 10 percent of African Americans have at least 50% European ancestry (equivalent of one parent) (Gates discovered that he himself is one of these)

- And 5 percent of African Americans have at least 12.5% Native American ancestry (equivalent to one great-grandparent)

Moreover, the average African American possesses around 18% European ancestry, according to molecular anthropologist, Mark D. Shriver. In terms of arithmetic mean, out of all of the 128 ancestors of the average African American, 106 are African and 22 are European. By contrast, European Americans possess overwhelmingly less racial admixture. The average Caucasian American only possesses a mere 0.7% African ancestry, which is the equivalent of having 127 white forebears and one African among all of one's 128 ancestors. Furthermore, 70% of Caucasian Americans have no African ancestors at all, and the 30% that do only possess around a mere 2.3% African ancestry (that is, out of all of one's 128 ancestors—125 European, and three African) (Sailer). This is proof that African Americans are, in general terms, mixed-race to a very considerable degree and that Caucasian Americans are chiefly European in actual terms. One of the prevailing factors behind the fact that a minority of Caucasians possess fractions of African blood is due to the "passing" phenomenon within the African-American community. It is estimated that as many as ten- to twenty-thousand African Americans were passing for white every year for the first two decades of the 1900s (Williamson 1980). Moreover, Gates even concluded in 2009 that, "African Americans ... are a racially mixed or mulatto people—deeply and overwhelmingly so."

In order to perpetuate white domination throughout antiquity, both in regard to population majority, as well as economic and socio-political superiority, those who possessed only partial European ancestry were consigned to the socially subordinate group. In the case of those of black-white mixes, these mixed-race individuals were susceptible and liable to social, political and economic inferiority due to their blackness alone. It is very much a historical and contemporary actuality in America that one is whatever makes him or her not white. As a result, several waves of movements have come and gone in order to challenge such a socio-racial norm in the United States. Beginning in the late 1970s and enduring onward through the twenty-first century, advocates of a new "biracial" movement attempted to set new societal standards in regard to how offspring of interracial relationships were to be socially perceived and regarded. An underlying reason as to why biracial movements have not had a lasting impact on changing the tides of society in regard to race is due to the fact that, as of yet, there is a lack of a community within American society where products of interracial unions form any sense of camaraderie in regard to kinship on the basis of their shared first-generational admixture. Furthermore, another answer to the lingering mystery as to why a biracial movement has not yet "stuck" lies in the societal pressures of race that America still imposes on its citizenry.

Nevertheless, there have been momentous pressures by those of multiracial heritage to gain social acceptance as people of multiracial descent. These persons feel that they are not acknowledging themselves in full if they are consigned to the identity of a race for which they feel they are not fully part of on the mere grounds of their multi-ethnicity. Because of the fact that biracial individuals possess a white parent, those proponents of a biracial movement challenge the fact that biracial individuals of black-white mixes are seen and socially accepted as black people. The overarching dilemma facing those who argue for a biracial movement is rooted in the existential reality of global racism. Racism is the coalescence of prejudice and power, and the power to adversely affect and impact another group is yielded from the access to resources coupled with prejudice because of race. Since white people do not see, perceive, or socially accept people of mixed-race as white, then that means that that person of mixed-race is vulnerable, susceptible, and liable to white racism, prejudice and discrimination. In regard to discrimination against those Americans of black African descent, discriminatory measures are a direct application of white power because of white prejudice.

In essence, it is because of a mixed-race person's blackness that he or she is discriminated against by Whites, and, as a just response to such inequality, that mixed-race person is afforded the protection against such white discriminatory measures also due to his or her blackness. It is imperative to come to the understanding that the whole point of a biracial identity is futile because an assertion of such a self-identification is an eradication and erosion of the protection of the maintenance of the civil liberties afforded him or her because of his or her membership, either in whole or in part, to the historically discriminated-against group. In America, the concept of race has, throughout antiquity, been very much rooted in the privileges and penalties based upon the perceived notions of one's appearance; and the assertion of a mixed-race identity merely serves individualistic interests, rather than eradicating general dilemmas in regard to those who, either in whole or in part, belong to minority racial and/or ethnic groups.

Such a verbal self-identification does nothing to propel the larger anti-racist movement, and it is simply a way of opting out of blackness solely for the individualistic advantage of being seen as something other than black. Verily, such an identity has little or nothing to do with dismantling white racism and supremacy. In fact, it plays into the hands of white racial superiority—because such mixed-race persons are looking to their white heritage to, in essence, break away from blackness; while, in reality, in an effort to weaken their affiliation and kinship to Blacks, they are weakening their very own disposition in the face of society, because, by a Eurocentric estimation, they are, and will always remain, whatever makes them non-white. And it is because of the existence of such racist mentalities, and the understanding that our society is not yet equal that the current system of racial classifications must be accepted as a means of accordingly advancing through such societal classifications.

On the 2010 United States census, a prominent man who was the son of a white woman from Kansas and a black man from Kenya checked "Black/African American/Negro." He, being of biracial descent, had the option of expressing himself in all of his racial complexity by checking "black" and "white," or simply "other." However, despite all of these multiple options, he checked solely "black," and left it at that. This man is the forty-fourth United States president, Barack Obama (born 1963). Obama is the first person of African-American descent to receive a nomination from a major American political party for President, and he is also the first individual of African-American descent to be elected President of the United States of America. Coupled with his wife, Michelle Obama (née Robinson) (born 1964) who is also of African-American descent and two daughters, Obama's immediate family is not only the first African-American first family, but also the first family of predominantly African descent to head any of the world's major industrialized democracies. Be as it may, several questions arise as to why a person of multiracial descent such as Obama would choose only one "race" on the census even though he is made up of more than one. Advocates of the multiracial movement, such as Elizabeth Chang (a Caucasian editor for the Washington Post married to a man of Asian descent), were frustrated that Obama "did not get with their multiracial program" (www.theroot.com).

Such an option to select multiple races on the census beginning in the year 2000 was seen as a monumental step towards progress in the biracial and multiracial movement. However, such a purportedly great leap forward is marred by the fact that discrimination still exists. In exemplification of this, a re-tabulation process occurs when people check more than one box on the census. An individual who checks both "white" and "black" is re-tabulated as a black person by the United States Census Bureau in order to protect that person against the discrimination that they might face for being a member, either in whole or in part, to that race. This is largely due to the fact that one cannot be protected from discrimination by being "mixed-race."

Verily, it is the understanding that history plays a vital role on the present that perpetuates race itself. The one-drop rule lives on because of the fact that the entire African-American ethnic group has been affected by it, and without the legacy of this "rule," then there would be very few people who could be veritably classified as "black." In large part, it is the legacy of the one-drop rule that consigns people of mixed-race heritage to a black socio-racial designation; however, it is the same rule that helped to not only establish, but also solidify, a community of people who shared a common heritage whose bloodlines had been racially diverse for generations. For "mixed-race" persons of recent admixture to gain social solidarity as an identifiable group, the "one-drop rule" must be repealed in regard to standards set by society. However, for such a rule to have its true repeal, one must be willing to acknowledge that virtually most African Americans are truly not "black" at all, as most of this group had historically faced the socio-racial dilemmas that current biracial individuals are, as a mixed-race people, striving to bring about an end to in this current day and age.

In general terms, biracial individuals of recent black-white mixes are striving to not only develop, but bring about a new societal norm in regard to socio-racial associations. Verily, people develop a culture of problem-solving regardless of whether or not it fits societal norms of culture. A "biracial" movement is a way of striving to solve the problem yielded from a mixed-race individual feeling detached from embracing his or her whole identity. However, mainstream values that are superimposed upon western society bar such a movement from impacting the mainstream values of racial identity. Throughout antiquity and modernity alike, myths, legends, and worldviews were methods that were used to solve a great deal of the problems that were, and continue to be, brought forth from technology-based innovations. This tactic is part of ceremony. Emerging in the middle twentieth century, social anthropology entailed that culture is a set of values. And those values that demarcate black from white and white from black perpetuate the irrelevance of an in-between social distinction such as "biracial," as well as the socio-political distinctions between black and white—encompassing in them the respective inequalities between Whites and Blacks.

In striving to substantiate the status quo of black socio-political and economic inequality with white people, three schools of thought emerged in bringing about reasoning to such disparities between Whites and Blacks. Those schools were the Jensen School, the Chicago School, and the Moynihan School. The Jensen School assessed that there were unequal intelligence levels between Whites and Blacks. This is, in essence, an intelligence quotient-based theory. The Chicago School asserted that there were issues of education and experience that explicated income inequalities between Whites and Blacks. This is essentially an education-based theory. And the Moynihan School stated that culture difference between Blacks and Whites ultimately cause discrimination and various "tastes for discrimination," which entail the willingness to adversely affect out of the impetus of discriminatory preferences. Culture biases, such as notions that Blacks value education less, set them up to have less equal opportunities in comparison to Whites, according to the Moynihan School. In line with such principles, values that validate the "culture of poverty" line of thought include the economy of the inner-city African American. In such an economy, these urban individuals feel that their dress, namely sagging, works for them in solving the various problems that they face in their community.

Another cultural peculiarity within the African-American community that assists in such inequality with Whites is, according to several sociologists and anthropologists, father absence. Such paternal absence is generated by a lack of familial stability ultimately established through fragmented ruptures originally brought about by the economy of slavery within the African-American community. During the various slave auctions of the Antebellum South, families were broken up for the sole purpose of the economic, social, and political benefit of the potential slaveholder and his property. This father absence ideal is further upheld by the Moynihan School for substantiating a culture of poverty argument, which was, in turn, largely inspired by the studies of Oscar Lewis (1914-1970). In his book, "Five Families: Mexican Case Studies in the Culture of Poverty," Lewis took note of the fact that Mexican families attained a sense of helplessness, inferiority, lack of awareness of history, and lack of awareness in regard to class consciousness. Verily, such ideals are not at all inconsistent with the plight of the African American under his former slave condition which is prescribed to the "culture of poverty" ideological framework.

However, some, including Booker T. Washington himself, ironically cited such slave conditions as an underlying factor behind African Americans comprising the most advanced Blacks in the world. Washington once stated that "the Negro did gain certain benefits from slavery." Those among these benefits, per Washington, included self-discipline and future-oriented values. Such benefits were, according to Washington, largely abandoned due to the existentialities of the Postbellum South—for the Reconstruction era amplified African Americans' sense of "present-orientedness" through allowing American Blacks to start "at the top instead of at the bottom," and to seek "a seat in Congress … [rather] than real estate or industrial skill." Washington declared that "it is vastly more important that we be prepared for the exercise of these privileges," when prompted to acknowledge the importance of legal rights granted during the postbellum era of the South (Cherry 1123).

By my own estimation, it is virtually nonsensical to conclude that African Americans served as beneficiaries to a slave system whose sole purpose was to humiliate the black race through exploiting such peoples and their resources, tools, and skills that they originally brought from Africa. Future-oriented values were virtually non-existent—for even Frederick Douglass himself remarked that the essential nature of slavery encompassed coercion, belonging to another person, and hopelessness for mobility or change. Verily, it is impossible to develop any values oriented toward future self-betterment when there is a very prevalent presence of hopelessness for mobility or change greatly spurred by white racial, social, economic, and political oppression. Even during the postbellum era of the South, the most prolific of those of African descent were still second-class citizens despite laws and militia presence that were active in striving to bring about any semblance of equality with Whites.

The end of the antebellum era and the dawning of the postbellum era did not signify universal white sympathetic sentiment toward black people; it did signify, however, the ineptitude of the slavery political system as an adequate way to propel the American economy forward. There was always at least some recognition among American Whites that black people were not property (as they were regarded in slavery), but people. The postbellum era of the South marked the full-fledged effort of American Whites to acknowledge such a just reality. Blacks were not at all treated preferentially during the Postbellum South as Washington surmised—it just marked the first time in history that African Americans were given the socio-political recognition that they were due as a people and as citizens of these United States of America. Perhaps such drastic socio-political standing from the slave plantation to the gubernatorial mansion (as P. B. S. Pinchback achieved for African Americans) might have been processed by many, including Washington himself, as a mark of "preferential treatment," but, then again, such advancement exposes the true subordinate state of the American Black during slavery, and, therewith, debunks any notion of slave status being "beneficial."

Perhaps the true reasoning behind Washington citing slavery as beneficial for African Americans lies in slavery's requisite for the black individual to acquiesce to white dominion. As Robert Cherry exclaims,

> Washington did…believe that African Americans were culturally inferior to Whites. He [1970, 74] contrasted the "semi-barbarous" African race with the White race that had attained "the highest civilization that the world knows." [Ultimately,] Washington [1970, 16] believed that the African culture was at a lower stage of development than European society.

Since Washington believed that white culture was superior to black culture, it was only fitting of him to conclude that white societal institutions, even the ones that were as vile as slavery itself, benefitted Blacks, nonetheless. And, per Washington, it was only when Blacks learned to submit to white culture that they could truly advance as a people. However, such acquiescence does nothing to advance the black race—because the whole objective behind

Eurocentric ceremony is to maintain white power by decimating any potential acquisition of power by Blacks or any other racial or ethnic group. Ironically enough, one of these tactics of decimating other groups by Whites and propelling their own maintenance of power was, in fact, the slavery political system. As Frederick Douglass once stated:

> Power concedes nothing without a demand. It never did and it never will. Find out just what any people will quietly submit to and you have found out the exact measure of injustice and wrong which will be imposed upon them, and these will continue till they are resisted with either words or blows, or both. The limits of tyrants are prescribed by the endurance of those whom they oppress.

Such black submissiveness is the legacy of the institution of slavery. A case in point of such acquiescence is the continued use of the term "nigger" or its successive variant, "nigga" within the African-American community. The word "nigga" is a term used in African American Vernacular English that began as an eye dialect form of the word "nigger," which is ultimately derived in turn from the Latin word, "niger," meaning the color black. "Nigger" was used throughout the slavery era of the United States as a contemptuous identification for a planter's slave property. Eventually, the word seeped into black culture as a way for African Americans to identify themselves. However, such a word that has, in the twenty-first century, become a term of endearment within the African-American community finds its original roots in the colonial racial oppression of enslaved black peoples.

It seems very much so that the white culture of the Antebellum South has not only lived on, but has also adversely impacted the culture within the African-American community—for contemporary Blacks see positivity in a word that was originally used as a means of denigrating the entire black race. Such is the legacy of slavery, and it also serves as proof that adopting white culture (whether antiquated or modern), as Washington suggestively advises, does not necessarily propel Blacks forward. In fact, it very well might hold them back. Some may argue that such a resulting outcome might be the whole point of Eurocentric ceremony, and the fact that African Americans perceive the term "nigger" as something positive only perpetuates Eurocentric notions and ideals that Blacks are innately inferior. By embracing inferiority, one becomes that which is inferior. So, welcoming white racist terms historically engendered to denounce— nigger—perpetuates and even validates that which was originally intended to be denounced (the quote-on-quote "nigger"). This actuality is a central reason behind the National Association for the Advancement of Colored People (NAACP) officially condemning the usage of both "nigga" and "nigger" in the twenty-first century.

Upon its original inception in 1909, the NAACP, which served as the successor organization to the Niagara Movement, intended, under the guidance of W. E. B. Du Bois, to do that which Booker T. Washington could not promise to the African-American people— emphasize the importance of civil rights for the American of black African descent. Much in line with the mentality of Frederick Douglass before him, Du Bois insisted that academic education, unwavering agitation, and socio-political activism would be the only way in which African Americans could achieve equality with Whites—counteracting John R. Commons' assessment. As Douglass once stated:

> Those who profess to favor freedom and yet depreciate agitation are people who want crops without ploughing the ground; they want rain without thunder and lightning; they want the ocean without the roar of its many waters. The

struggle may be a moral one, or it may be a physical one, or it may be both. But it must be a struggle.

In his orations, Douglass urged the African American to endure through the struggle of withstanding Whites' imposition of black disfrashisement, societal segregation and economic inferiority. Even before white supremacy ran rampant throughout the South— decimating any advancement gained by Americans of black African descent, Douglass advocated for not only the black vote, but also the female vote. In a speech given on November 15, 1867, Douglass declared, "A man's rights rest in three boxes. The ballot box, jury box and the cartridge box. Let no man be kept from the ballot box because of his color. Let no woman be kept from the ballot box because of her sex." Just sixteen years prior to this speech, Sojourner Truth, a black former slave to a Dutch planter, was invited to speak in the 1851 Akron, Ohio conference on Women's Rights, and she orated the famous "Ain't I A Woman" speech which manifested her accordance with Africana womanism principles as well as her affinity to being black before being a woman. As Truth orated in her momentous speech, "That man over there says that women need to be helped into carriages, and lifted over ditches, and to have the best place everywhere. Nobody ever helps me into carriages, or over mud-puddles, or gives me any best place! And ain't I a woman?"

In recognition of her priority of race, followed by class, and then gender, Sojourner Truth conveyed that black women could not afford to be at odds with black men, because, in weakening the disposition of black men, they were, in turn, weakening the disposition of black people in general (Hudson-Weems). Because many white women, including those who attended this 1851 conference, felt that they should be given the vote before black men, they became feminists as well as racists, due to the fact that they emphasized gender first, then class, followed by race in terms of how they felt that their voice should be heard in regard to mainstream societal ideals. Many of them became opposed to abolitionism during the antebellum era of the South, and, propelled by the advancement of the black man before their own as white women, they became avid racists who defended white racial supremacy ensuing the Civil War and postbellum eras.

Verily, Du Bois deemed that the abject condition of the African American was largely due to their inadequacies during the Postbellum South. According to Du Bois, the disadvantaged state of the African American after the postbellum era was largely due to the economic ineptitude of African Americans. By the estimation of Du Bois, the rise of white supremacist groups like the Ku Klux Klan, the White League, and the Red Shirts and their subsequent Jim Crow laws, was conceived out of class issues rather than socio-racial ones. In his book, "Black Reconstruction in America," Du Bois cites the division of white and black laborers as the impetus behind the failure to impact the socio-economic superstructure that was ruled by the "white propertied class." However, such an issue of classism involved other groups other than the black and white laboring class and the white propertied class. Be as it may, a black middle class had already long been formulated that was persistent in striving to bring about black-white socio-political and economic equality.

In fact, Du Bois' own family was part of such a class—for Du Bois had been born to a mother whose family consisted of African, Dutch, and English ancestors who had been free for generations in Great Barrington, Massachusetts. Du Bois' father, much like his wife, had also been born free predating the American Revolution, and he was also descended from Africans as well as French Huguenots. These African Americans who were free before the Civil War had long been active in doing just what Du Bois cited that the black and white laboring classes should have purportedly done—end white economic, social, political, and racial supremacy. It was very much the case that, during the Postbellum South, this largely mixed-race or "mulatto" elite had largely been second-class citizens, but they were not the most inferior class during the socio-political hierarchy of the postbellum era, however—for that place had been left for the newly-freed bondspersons in the three-tier stratified society of the Postbellum South. In fact, Du Bois' own moniker for this mulatto elite would later manifest itself in what he called the "Talented Tenth."

Verily, this group was to serve as the legacy of such a postbellum mulatto class, and Du Bois' own goal for such a group was that they, through their exquisite college-educated intellect, carve out a means of equality with Whites by leading the black masses through the example that they were to set themselves. However, it is, even in today's societal context, very much a necessity that the African-American community be united through class means. Only then can social, political, and economic oppression motivated by race be eliminated. In capitalist principle, classism generally refers to the amount of income one makes. This is opposed to Marxism, where classism concerns ownership of production. Both principles, however, reflect the disadvantageous position of the American of black African descent—for, as aforementioned, over 25% of African Americans subsist below the poverty line and the median net worth of African-American families is $10,000, which is over $70,000 less than the average white family.

Such class inequality is very much a socio-racial epidemic. As some Blacks have been able to ascend into a lifestyle that is unlike that of the black masses, they have abandoned an abject community of black people that are consigned to disadvantaged conditions. In more ways than one, American society has been stratified in a way in which it was stratified in the nineteenth century—most black people are at the bottom of the three-tier society, while some Blacks are afforded considerably more privilege than the black masses, and white people generally comprise the executive status of society. The remedy to such inequality is not necessarily intermarriage or "crossbreeding" as John R. Commons once asserted. White blood does not, has not, and never will necessarily empower the African American. Only integrated class, socio-political, economic and educational ideals will bring light to the African-American community, which will, in turn, eliminate the notion that there needs to be a "biracial" community in society. Alas, such a community will only play into the hands of Eurocentric dominion and will do nothing to mobilize a seemingly shiftless mass of impoverished people of black African descent in these United States of America.

Chapter VI: "The People, Custom, and Class Comprising the
Postbellum South Mulattoes and Their Legacy"

Indeed, the forerunner to what W. E. B. Du Bois called the "Talented Tenth" of the African-American community was in fact the mulatto elite of the Postbellum South. They were the illustrious Creoles of color like the family of Homer Plessy; they were the slave-owning Free Negroes of Charleston, South Carolina; and they were the very own forebears of Du Bois himself that comprised the very small free black population in New England and the Middle Atlantic states. These persons of color had acquired wealth long before the emancipation of bondspersons in 1865, and they became the models of what a competent American black population could be and could become in the imminent and distant futures. This mulatto elite would later go on to serve as the precursor to the contemporary black middle class of America. Historically, many of these mulattoes of the Postbellum South were as fervent in defending slavery as the staunch white supremacists of the antebellum era, because they had become beneficiaries of such a system, and social and political capital was built through the maintenance of such a politico-economic system.

Such social stratification, or the status process of society, was not at all inconsistent with the mulatto elite of colonial French America—most notably the colony of Saint-Domingue, which now comprises the independent nation of Haiti. The *gens de couleur libres*, or free people of color of this French colony, were, in order to bask in the economic glory of France's most prized colonial possession, committed to align themselves in regard to social standing with the *grand blancs*, or white plantation class, and these free people of color were in accord with the advocacy of the continuation of slavery—much like the Free Negroes of the Antebellum Southern United States. In fact, Julien Raimond, a mulatto indigo planter, claimed that he owned "one-third of all the slaves in the colony" (Popkin). This was simply a blatant attempt to be equitable with the *grand blancs* and make mulattoes more aloof with their black cousins.

However, rather than receiving more acceptance from the *grand blancs*, many mulattoes were subject to public humiliation and second-class citizenship, as was the case in the United States during the time. However, race was always linked with social class— regardless of the European colonial possession in question. Because of the fact that Guadeloupe was the least prosperous French colonial possession, it was long rumored that the ruling propertied class there was not pure European at all. This was a substantiation of the correlation of race and social status within the lens of Eurocentric ideals. For instance, because Guadeloupe lagged behind all other French colonies, its backwardness was attributed to purported "black rule" there. As such, the *grand blancs* of Martinique would tell persons behind the hand that all the alleged Whites of Guadeloupe were not pure French at all—but, rather, just really light colored people (Miller 207-08).

Nevertheless, the mulatto elite of the United States and the Latin American colonies was not only able to survive, but also thrive because of the endogamous nature of such a community of persons. They maintained their lot in society by explicitly marrying within their own circles, and aloofness was established in regard to contact with darker-skinned people. Associations, institutions, and communities were also selective in exclusivity, and many major American urban centers were well known for their exclusive mulatto circles including Chicago, Harlem, and Los Angeles. Other cities were also notorious for their exclusivity based on the premise of the fairness of one's skin complexion including Atlanta, Boston, Charleston, Louisville, Nashville, New Orleans, New York, Philadelphia, and, most scrupulously, Washington, D. C. (Khanna

34). One individual of color who was part of the previously-mentioned "Blue Vein" Society once declared,

> We people of mixed blood are ground between the upper and the nether millstone. Our fate lies between absorption by the white race and extinction in the black. The one doesn't want us yet, but may take us in time. The other would welcome us, but it would be for us a backward step. 'With malice towards none, with charity for all,' we must do the best we can for ourselves and those who are to follow us. Self-preservation is the first law of nature (Chestnutt).

Verily, the height of the mulatto elite reached its zenith during the postbellum era of the South, and the response of the mulatto to the end of slavery was to demarcate the light-complected from the darker-complected. This is what established the three-tier society that had been both present and prevalent during the slavery era. As previously mentioned, slavery was done away with out of economic reasons, and with such a shift in the political economy, much of the mulatto elite of the former French colony of Saint-Domingue as well as the Southern United States had to find new ways to maintain their social standing. It was very much the case that the peak of the extent of power of the postbellum mulatto was during the period from 1865-1877—for many of the rights that were denied to these persons of color in other times throughout history were briefly granted during this postbellum period. Verily, such an existentiality yielded a three-tier system where the mulatto elite stood above the bondspersons and below the white propertied class. Nonetheless, the opportunism of mixed-race men like P. B. S. Pinchback served as proof of the affluent wellbeing of the mulatto during this era. Although the mulatto of the Antebellum South was afforded a lifestyle congruent with the slave-owning propertied white class, the postbellum mulatto was granted economic, political and social standing not too dissimilar to Whites in any era. In 1893, P. B. S. Pinchback eventually rose to the pinnacle of the ranks of the mulatto elite after he moved to Washington, D. C. and he subsequently joined the upper echelons of these social circles based on skin tone among persons of color. However, none of the privileges and *mode de vie* that he enjoyed during this timeframe was comparable to the socio-political status afforded to him during the postbellum era.

In his book, "Black Reconstruction in America," Du Bois cites the lack of solidarity between the black and white laboring classes as instrumental in the rise of white supremacist factions in the South. Du Bois believed that such a unification by class means would bring about an end to the dominion of the "white propertied class." By my estimation, it was, as Du Bois asserts, advantageous for African Americans to build solidarity through class means, because only then could social, political, and economic oppression motivated by race be eliminated. However, there was, even during this time period, very much so a "black" or "mulatto propertied class" that was fighting to build about wholesale, long-lasting social equality with white people during the postbellum era of the South. Their interests were arguably just as important as those of the laboring class in repressing the white supremacist dynamic that was growing during the postbellum era and that manifested itself in full force ensuing the postbellum era. Such a tour de force by white supremacist organizations gave way to their imposition of a binary, or two-tier, system that entailed the subordination of any and all persons of black African descent.

Although only in part, the ineptitude of the mulatto elite of the time was largely due to their own exclusivity. These persons of color were not at all aligned ideologically with the newly freed bondspersons, and intermarriage, as aforementioned, between these mulatto elite and the formerly enslaved was, although legal, regarded as social taboo and was rarely done. Such exclusivity and lack of solidarity between all persons of black African descent yielded the facility of white supremacist organizations to consign all of those of black African descent to second-class citizenship and subordination after the postbellum era. In the slavery era of the United States, the mulatto elite would vest their wealth into striving to prove that they were of no less socio-economic stock than white slaveholders. These attempts by the mulatto elite are largely made manifest through what is now considered conspicuous consumption—a term first coined by nineteenth- and twentieth-century economist, Thorstein Veblen (1857-1929). By my estimation, it was because of lack of common ideological interests between the mulatto elite of the Postbellum South and the newly-freed bondspersons that facilitated the denigration of both groups by white supremacist factions, which gave way to Jim Crow laws and societal segregation.

However, although civil cases like *Plessy v. Ferguson* institutionally legalized segregation and gave way to Jim Crow laws throughout the South, there were certain enclaves within the African-American community in particular that thrived—so much to the point where such communities rivaled those where Whites lived. During the second decade of the twentieth century, the community of Greenwood, which was located within the city limits of Tulsa, Oklahoma, the black community there became very much self-reliant, and they had established flourishing businesses, schools, shops, and residential areas. Industry and commerce also thrived in this exclusive African-American community, and, because such a community of African Americans had prospered, coupled with the growing white supremacist factions active in the area, Whites were aiming to end such black economic prosperity, which was rapidly developing the moniker of "The Negro Wall Street."

Many of the residents of Greenwood were part of the professional and bureaucratic class, or black middle class; but such upward social mobility occurred not because of generational endowment inherited from antebellum mulattoes, but rather because of the solidarity of the community as a whole during that time period. Ironically enough, due to the restrictions of African Americans and where they could invest their pecuniary capital, societal segregation had established the resurgence of black business—especially in this community of Greenwood, Tulsa, Oklahoma. There was no competition amongst the black and white businesses because African Americans could not vest any of their finances in white-owned businesses due to the circumstances exacerbated by Jim Crow laws and societal segregation. In such an instance, African Americans had multiplied on their own political and economic power by distributing and concentrating their wealth within their very own communities. Whereas the mulatto elite of the Postbellum South were practicing conspicuous consumption to gain some semblance of equality with Whites during the nineteenth century, the African-American community in Greenwood was looking amongst themselves and their own to build and maintain social and political capital—which established self-betterment and self-empowerment for not only the community, but for African Americans as a whole.

As aforementioned, many of these professional and bureaucratic African Americans of Greenwood were not descended from the mulatto elite of the Postbellum South. Rather, these doctors, lawyers, dentists and clergymen were descended from the original "Exodusters," or those African Americans who left the Old South to free themselves from staunch white racial oppression. During this time, there were a little over a dozen well-known African-American physicians residing within the Greenwood community. One of them, Dr. A. C. Jackson was touted as "the most able Negro doctor in

America" by the Mayo Clinic. In order to sustain white racial superiority throughout the South, many white supremacists groups like the Ku Klux Klan commonly carried out lynchings, arson on edifices within the black community, and several other means of terror. Notwithstanding, these atrocities were also experienced firsthand by my very own ancestors, including my maternal great-grandfather, L. E. Patterson. As many African-American families continued to grow weary of such oppression, they began some of the first mass migration movements out of the Old South and into states like Kansas, Colorado, and Oklahoma—including the all-black community of Greenwood, Tulsa, Oklahoma. In other instances, African Americans established all-black towns in rural places within the Old South; one of these establishments within the South included Eatonville, Florida—which went on to become one of the first all-black towns to be incorporated in the United States. Other notable Exoduster settlements included Nicodemus and Quindaro, which were both located within the state of Kansas.

Nevertheless, prominent African-American leader, Frederick Douglass, had, near the end of his life, opposed the Exoduster movement which later went on to produce communities like "The Black Wall Street." He advised African Americans to, through avid agitation, "stick it out" with regard to fighting white racial oppression in the Old South. However, as African Americans journeyed on to build self-empowerment by establishing autonomous all-black communities like Greenwood, Whites inauspiciously eyed such efforts as the black community grew stronger through such solidarity. As the local Klansmen chapter in Tulsa, Oklahoma grew to over three-thousand members by the early 1920s, the white population moved to end black socio-economic prosperity in the area. As Dr. A. C. Jackson was shot to death after exiting his front porch, the Tulsa Race Riots began, which effectively ended "The Black Wall Street" era of Greenwood, Tulsa, Oklahoma. In this instance, the African-American community of Greenwood suffered thirty-nine fatalities amidst eight-hundred wounded, and the community, in all of its once thriving commercial, residential, and industrial presence, was left in ruins as if it were a battleground of war.

Such devastation of black prosperity is yet another signification of Whites' mentality in regard to empowerment of persons of black African descent. Such empowerment should not and will not exist because, per Eurocentric ideals, African-descended people are inferior; and anything repudiating such an ideal must be decimated—as was the case with "The Black Wall Street." Be as it may, even the most brilliant of African Americans withstood white racism. W. E. B. Du Bois, a gilded African-American leader who earned degrees from Fisk University, the University of Berlin, and a Ph.D. from Harvard University, could not find work despite all of his academic achievement. In lieu of such unfortunate circumstances centering on his black heritage, he relocated to Philadelphia, Pennsylvania and published "The Philadelphia Negro," which went on to become one of the very first statistically-based studies on urban sociology. He drew inspiration from the works of British social researcher Charles Booth (1840-1916). Booth conducted studies on the class stratification of the city of London called, "Life and Labour of the People of London."

Du Bois' findings in "The Philadelphia Negro" revealed the social, political, and economic disparities between the African-American populace of Philadelphia and the white areas of the city. There existed a stark contrast between the African-American Philadelphian and the persons of color in "The Black Wall Street." Although reaching its peak of prosperity several decades later, "The Black Wall Street" evinced that, if Blacks relied on themselves with regard to concentrating their assets, such focal concentration would improve the social, political, and economic condition of the African-American community as a whole. This was, alas, not at all the case in Philadelphia, and, as so, African Americans there were, in general, socio-economically inferior to white Philadelphians. Of course, there were minor exceptions due to the fact that some of the best-off African-American families had been afforded socio-economic privilege that had been present in those respective families for many generations (as with the mulatto elite). However, prosperity spread throughout an entire community of African-American Philadelphians was non-existent due to the lack of solidarity that had been strongly developed in places like "The Black Wall Street."

Verily, a "Black Wall Street" was able to develop due to the fact that these persons of African-American descent in Greenwood, Tulsa, Oklahoma oriented themselves toward their commonality of black heritage shared among them. This was not always the case in regard to those of wholly African descent and those of only partial African descent. Oftentimes, custom was centered on the quantifying of white heritage among African-descended persons that determined not only one's lot in society with regard to white people, but also one's standing within the African-American community at large. Many African-American leaders saw the backwardness of such a custom; W. E. B. Du Bois even remarked that it was necessary to "class those of African descent together" concerning the census designation of a "mulatto" race.

Historically, the term "mulatto" varied drastically in meaning throughout American antiquity. In addition to being a reference to those of mixed African and European ancestry, it was also used to identify those of any mixed ancestry—including progeny of unions between Whites and Native Americans, Whites and South Asians, as well as African Americans and Native Americans. Even some Native American groups themselves self-identified as mulatto, as was the case with the Inocoplo tribe. Alas, the Hening's Statutes of Virginia 1705 stated the following:

> And for clearing all manner of doubts which hereafter may happen to arise upon the construction of this act, or any other act, who shall be accounted a mulatto, Be it enacted and declared, and it is hereby enacted and declared, That the child of an Indigenous and the child, grand child, or great grand child, of a negro shall be deemed, accounted, held and taken to be a mulatto.

However, by the middle of the nineteenth century, the terminology "mulatto" had considerably shifted in regard to meaning and designation, and new classifications were introduced that quantified black ancestry within the scope of a mixed-race person's entire ancestral lineage. In the census year 1890, a racial reorganization had taken place:

> Be particularly careful to distinguish between blacks, mulattoes, quadroons, and octoroons. The word "black" should be used to describe those persons who have three-fourths or more black blood; "mulatto," those persons who have from three-eighths to five-eighths black blood; "quadroon," those persons who have one-fourth black blood; and "octoroon," those persons who have one-eighth or any trace of black blood (Hochschild).

Although these "race"-based classifications were rigid in regard to definitive, *de jure* characteristics, they were, in *de facto* terms, rooted in impressions based on skin complexion rather than explicit information regarding ancestry; and, as so, instructions were lacking concerning how these ancestral fractions would be determined and tabulated. It was indeed the case that perception regarding a mixed-race person's heritage led to falsities and inaccuracies with regard to statistical data gathered from census information. Josephine Ford, my

 paternal great-great-grandmother was a full-blooded Cherokee woman; however, she was tabulated as a "mulatto" on the 1910 and 1920 United States censuses. Her daughter, Etta Ford (my paternal great-grandmother), was listed on the 1910 census as a "mulatto" as well; whereas Etta's acute heritage encompassed a white father of predominantly German descent, Hillary Ford (my paternal great-great-grandfather) and her full-blooded Cherokee mother, Josephine Ford.

As aforementioned, society, not only in the United States, but also in other former European colonial possessions, was stratified in direct correlation to the quantifying of white heritage within an individual's full ancestral pedigree. As a result, hypodescent categorizations were meticulously stratified, and minute exceptions concerning one's heritage were scrupulously recorded due to the sole fact that civil liberties and duties were directly tied to the amount of white ancestry that an individual possessed. Be as it may, my paternal great-great-grandmother wanted her daughter, Etta Ford—my great-grandmother—to marry a Caucasian doctor from southern Alabama. Etta's father, Hillary Ford (my great-great-grandfather), was also, as aforementioned, white, and Josephine wanted her daughter to marry a Caucasian man just as she had done.

If Etta would have succumbed to her mother's will, she would have further increased her societal standing in the community and would have built further social and political capital for her mother's family—who were Cherokees. However, Etta wed a blue-eyed African-American man, Robert Hick Gantt—my paternal great-grandfather—who was also of mixed-race (of English, German, and African descent). Due to ongoing tension pertaining to the societal pressures provoked from such a union, my great-grandparents moved north to Pennsylvania, where my paternal grandmother, Tresia Marie McClain (née Gantt) was born on March 12, 1928. There, my great-grandfather, Robert Hick Gantt, became very active in the African-American ecclesiastic community, and he eventually, as previously mentioned, went on to become an ordained minister in the African Methodist Episcopal Church of Zion denomination and was active in ministry in Westmoreland County, Pennsylvania during much of the twentieth century.

In many more ways than one, white supremacy throughout the South incited migration movements of African Americans out of the Old South—as was with the case of the immediate family of my paternal great-grandfather, Robert Hick Gantt as well as my maternal great-grandfather, L. E. Patterson; and such white racial oppression throughout antiquity that many African Americans faced, including my own ancestors, facilitated the development of a black community in addition to the steady accretion of the former mulatto elite into such a black community. The legacy of the postbellum mulatto and his societal standing remains a vestigial remnant in regard to the contemporary African-American community. Perhaps it could be surmised that such an exclusive "mulatto" community was in fact the inhibitor of universal black progress across the board—for the powers that be allowed for a fraction of African-descended persons, the so-called "mulatto" elite, to attain some socio-political relevance in comparison to white people. It is very much so the case that this mulatto class were the ideal that the black masses were to emulate.

However, these persons of color were not at all the change that many wished to see in the world with regard to universal black progress. In a Eurocentric standard, they were the tokens; however, in an Africanist perspective, they were beacons of hope for black people everywhere.

In his own eyes, the postbellum mulatto held neither of those perspectives—because his standing in society was very much in line with the individualistic interest of him and him alone; and, for this reason, the prosperous postbellum mulatto was found far and few between in the scope of the mass of the black race. This soon led to complete invisibility in regard to the relevance of the postbellum mulatto throughout the annals of history due to the fact that this elite social class of a once three-tier American society became assimilated into the larger African-American community ensuing white supremacists' imposition of a binary system of society, which effectively ended the postbellum era outright. The mulatto elite had become neither absorbed into white socio-political circles nor extinct in the black masses, as the mulatto had dichotomously assumed before. Rather, these persons began to involve themselves in the socio-racial dilemmas pitted against all persons of color—regardless of white ancestry, and, as a result, the mulatto elite converged with darker Blacks for a common end-all objective—societal equality.

Chapter VII: "The Metamorphosis of Technology amidst the
Conservancy of Ceremony"

It is very much the case in regard to the social structure that the more things change, the more they remain the same. As previously introduced, there are two sides of the overall "coin" of culture—technology (an ever-changing concept consisting of societal tools and skills) and ceremony (a continuous constant entailing societal beliefs, rituals, and worldviews). Culture changes in response to the problems that humanity needs to solve. Although technology has metamorphosed throughout the centuries, the line of thought that constitutes the "ceremony" aspect of culture, particularly in the mainstream, has subsisted in the Western World despite technological advancement that has propelled western society forward.

In ideal terms, the progressive metamorphosis of technology should idyllically influence a shift in society's mainstream belief systems, because culture, which is part of social structure, is a toolkit for solving societal problems, and if those problems have been solved, then the worldviews embedded within culture should change as well. As people go about solving their problems, things that work should be valued, and things that do not should not be valued by my estimation. This existentiality comprises technology-based culture, and such a cultural system is the key to bringing about veritable social equality among the "races." However, we live in a ceremony-based culture—where things that are detrimental to advancement are still valued, and things that are necessary for advancement are, nonetheless, undervalued.

In the scope of western culture, a colonial mentality among people of color greatly contributes to internal colonialism. A colonial mentality entails the valuing of Eurocentric models of cultural institutions such as family, polity, economy, education, and religion over all other models of those various cultural institutions— particularly those of one's own cultural model. As such a colonial mentality comprises ceremony-based culture, this reverence of Eurocentric models is detrimental to black advancement due to the sole premise that black people are non-white, and exaltation of a group outside of their own detains any real progress for their own group in particular. This was one of the underlying problems of the mentality of the mulatto elite of the postbellum era—they were looking to whiteness all the while being denied by the very thing that they were looking towards. However, such a frame of mind can largely be attributed to the presence, both historically and concurrently, of white internal colonialism, which encompasses the presence of Whites as the dominant people and nation over subordinate ones in specific countries and territories throughout the Occident, or the Western World.

Verily, the superstructure consists of everything that is not part of the material world, including ideology, religion, and culture, and the superstructure is reflective to the economic base. The economic base includes the modes of production, or forces of production crucial to the maintenance and advancement of the political economy. According to twentieth-century German sociologist, Theodor Adorno (1903-1969), the overthrow of the current condition of the superstructure would eventually change the capitalist mode of production. In other words, Adorno believed that a change in ceremony would produce a change in technology. Essentially, those who manipulated the resource structure of society, namely Western Whites, also controlled the overarching superstructure encompassing those respective western societies.

In essence, the resource structure of society consists of dominion over resources coupled with the distribution of those particular resources, and resources are mediated through one's sense of agency. For instance, possessing the necessary resources, tools, and skills (technology), does not necessarily translate into the realization of a particular agenda. However, the lack of possession of the necessary resources, tools and skills (technology), almost always results in the failure to achieve any realistic agenda. Because people of black African descent lacked the access to such technology, they have, as a resulting factor, been adversely impacted by those who did have such access to technology. And since the societal superstructure has been manipulated by Eurocentric standards on the basis of white control over the resource structure, black people around the world have been enduring in a struggle to build any competitive relevance to white people in an apparently white-controlled social structure.

Per Adorno, a shift in Eurocentric-dominated worldviews in the mainstream would metamorphose the technologically-based system that propelled the overarching political economy. However, by my own estimation, white racism is not necessarily the impetus behind the capitalist mode of production. For, as aforementioned, the exploitation and denigration of the black "race" group did not emerge out of initial racist intentions, but rather out of economic ones. Although the superstructure of society and the economic base are interrelated due to the fact that the same powers are in control of both entities, the real root in the current-day socio-economic inequality among the "races" in the Western World is found in two distinct phenomena. White racism emerged out of self-reverence among white people in regard to their own customs, culture, traditions, and, particularly, appearance. This self-reverence gave way to contemptuous perceptions of other peoples whose societies did not fit their own customs, culture, traditions, and appearance. Such is the precursor to Eurocentrism. These prejudices would later manifest themselves in white racism only at the point in which Whites acquired the power to affect other groups outside of their own.

The plight of persons of color in regard to their lack of power within the scope of the political economy and the corresponding economic base is due to the mere fact that submissiveness of certain masses of people is necessary in order to propel the current politico-economic system forward—in both antiquity and modernity alike. In order to solidify the lots within society that these "masses" comprised, "race" emerged as an inhibitor in an effort to deny those who were not Western Whites from enjoying certain lifestyle standards afforded to those Western Whites. Although such lifestyle standards could not exist without the labor of the masses, these masses were barred from certain *modes de vie* afforded to Western Whites due to the fact that they were not part of the group of people that had conceived of such an agenda that yielded these particular *modes de vie* for these Western Whites. As a result, "race," as previously mentioned, emerged as a socio-political construct that was designed in an effort to bar certain individuals of the rights, privileges, and *modes de vie* that western white groups in particular enjoyed in overwhelmingly disproportionate excesses.

In defining race, intermingling between the various "races" had to be detained as well. In the United States, especially during the height of the Jim Crow era, anti-miscegenation laws, as they were ubiquitously called, were put in place in order to not only keep the races separate, but to also perpetuate the designation of persons of black African descent as inferior and second-class. The great majority of the states within the union barred intermingling between the races, and many statutes barred further relations between Whites and other groups—most notably Asians in California and the West Coast. Such measures like the anti-miscegenation laws were imprints of white dominion in not only the United States, but also in other parts of the Western World. In essence, what was occurring in the United States during the time was also the status quo in South Africa, Australia, and other parts of the world where Whites exercised power and control.

After centuries of oppression from Whites in the United States, African Americans were eventually moving to attain the rights that they had coveted to regain since the end of the postbellum era of the South. By the middle 1950s, African Americans had finally broken through one part of this Jim Crow system by legally defeating the system at the federal level through the victory in *Brown v. Board of Education* in 1954, which reversed previous precedent set forth by the "separate-but-equal" ruling in *Plessy v. Ferguson*. However, even despite this landmark case in 1954, there were still years of toil and strife to come for the African-American people to strive to truly overcome all parts of societal segregation and discrimination.

Be as it may, the events of the 1960s were devastating for the African-American community. In 1963 alone, Medgar Evers was gruesomely murdered in Mississippi and four black children perished in the 16th Street Baptist Church bombing in Birmingham, Alabama. These events went on to inspire legendary African-American singer-songwriter and pianist Nina Simone to conceive a musical composition based on the plight of the African-American people during this time. The song, titled "Mississippi Goddam," was released as a single and was subsequently boycotted in several Southern states, allegedly because of the inclusion of the word "goddam" in the title. However, most within the African-American community attributed its banning to the content within the song, particularly the onus that it placed on white terror as an inhibitor to universal black progress and prosperity everywhere.

Together with "Four Women" and "To Be Young, Gifted and Black," "Mississippi Goddam" was one of Simone's most famous protest compositions. In the lyrics of the song, Simone sojourns in congruence with the common consensus of the time that civil rights activists and other African Americans should "go slow" and incrementally make changes in the United States. As she sings, "Keep on sayin' 'go slow'… to do things gradually would bring more tragedy. Why don't you see it? Why don't you feel it? I don't know; I don't know. You don't have to live next to me—just give me my equality!" In essence, this line in the song conveys that some Blacks were not necessarily discontented with segregation—it was just the case that African Americans as a whole witnessed the blatant disparities between the white and black societies of the time which prompted many to believe that segregation was indeed "separate and unequal." For many like Nina Simone, this inequality was the catalyst for movements to change such an unjust status quo.

On the recording, Simone cynically announces the song as "a show tune, but the show hasn't been written for it yet." The song begins jauntily with a show tune feel, but it demonstrates its political focus early on with its chorus, "Alabama's got me so upset; Tennessee's made me lose my rest, and everybody knows about Mississippi goddam." Within white circles, the song was an embarrassingly all-time low for Simone as a recording artist; however, the black community felt a deep connection with both the song as well as Simone's conveyance of sentiments about the tumultuous times presented in front of the American people—particularly within the Southern United States during the Jim Crow era.

Verily, black civil rights agitation during the middle twentieth century was not limited to mere cultural activism such as the music of Nina Simone. In fact, several social and political organizations were being founded during the midst of the Jim Crow era in order to further increase the rights and civic privileges afforded to non-white persons, particularly African Americans. Using leaders like Dr. Martin Luther King, Jr. (1929-1968) and organizations such as King's own Southern Christian Leadership Conference (SCLC), as well as the Congress of Racial Equality (CORE), the Student Nonviolent Coordinating Committee (SNCC), and the previously-mentioned NAACP, African Americans as a people were moving to abolish racial segregation, disfranchisement, exploitation, and violence in the 1950s and 60s, which became known as the larger African-American Civil Rights Movement.

All persons of African descent nationwide were not yet free from the bonds of injustice; they were not yet freed from social and economic oppression. The African-American Civil Rights Movement succeeded in its immediate purpose to free all black citizens, regardless of geographic location, from malevolent oppression imposed by the social structure of the time. The movement went on to provide economic and political self-sufficiency, racial pride, and undiminished dignity within the greater African-American

community. In fact, slogans such as "black is beautiful" became commonplace and popular within the black community in striving to erode away standards based on Eurocentrism that had long plagued universal African-American progress.

Perhaps a changing in the tide of Africanist

perspectives among American people of African descent became most readily apparent with the mentalities of mixed-race individuals like Fredi Washington (1903-1994), an accomplished dramatic African-American film actress, and Walter White (1893-1955), an African-American civil rights activist who led the NAACP for nearly a quarter-century. Both were of mixed African-European ancestry and both could have easily assimilated into the white race as white people. However, they chose instead to defend their black racial identity alongside the black masses. In this instance, members of the once-exclusive mulatto elite who once self-segregated themselves from the black masses, had joined forces with the masses of black people to attain true equality within a white-dominated society. In fact, the true invisibility of the postbellum mulatto lies in the fact that these two groups of people—the mulatto and the predominant black—fused together under a common objective due to shared racial oppression from Whites that they both had endured throughout antiquity. This is indeed the juncture at which the "mulatto" became the "light-skinned Black."

Individuals like Fredi Washington and Walter White could have easily "passed" for white, or they could have, on the other hand, insisted on their mixed-race state of being, but they instead fought on as black people. And the

only minor detail that distinguished them from the general masses of black people was that their skin was light; but as socio-racial inequality subsisted, the value of such a complexion began to matter less and less. Walter White once said, "I am a Negro. My skin is white; my eyes are blue; my hair is blond. The traits of my race are nowhere visible upon me" (White 3). Five of Walter White's great-great-great-grandparents were black-identified and the other twenty-seven were Caucasian. Fredi Washington, an African-American film actress, also possessed high degrees of admixture with Europeans, and she showed a light complexion and blue-green eyes. Washington even portrayed a character named Peola in the 1934 Academy Award-nominated film, "Imitation of Life." Peola was a young African-American character who chose to pass for white in the face of white society. However, Washington herself was a staunch defender of her black identity and, in 1945, she stated,

> You see I'm a mighty proud gal, and I can't, for the life of me, find any valid reason why anyone should lie about their origin or anything else for that matter. Frankly, I do not ascribe to the stupid theory of white supremacy and to try to hide the fact that I am a Negro for economic or any other reasons; if I do, I would be agreeing to be a Negro makes me inferior...

Fredi Washington was offered superstardom—the level of contemporaries like Greta Garbo and Joan Crawford—on the sole condition that she deny her race and self-identify as a white actress. Fredi responded to such a dilemma by posing, "Why can't I be a Negro and be a star?" She refused to deny her race for wealth and star status. In her eyes, whiteness was not a determinant of social progress—neither individually nor holistically within the African-American community. On account of such a mentality, Washington founded the Negro Actors Guild in 1937 whose purpose was to bring about an end to discrimination as well as stereotypical casting of black actors in Hollywood.

Verily, individuals like Fredi Washington and Walter White defended their blackness due to white racial superiority and oppression that reigned supreme before the advent of the African-American Civil Rights Movement. In essence, their efforts were made so as to change the ceremony-based status quo of the time. Even as recent as 2009, ceremony centering on Eurocentric empowerment endures. On October 6, 2009, Keith Bardwell, a Justice of the Peace from Robert, Louisiana declined to officialize the marriage between Terence McKay, a young African American, and his Caucasian fiancée, Beth Humphrey. When prompted to bring about a validation behind his refusal to marry this interracial couple, Keith Bardwell exclaimed, "I'm not a racist...Most black society does not readily accept offspring of such relationships, and neither does white society...I don't want to put children in a situation they didn't bring on themselves. In my heart, I feel the children will later suffer" (Ellzey).

Verily, such an incident brings light to the fact that many still accept the reality of a segregated society entailing "white society" and a "black" one. Essentially, the very objective of minority rights movements within the United States and the world was to end segregation among the "races," because these various "societies" were not truly equal at all. It was long ago realized that, in order for persons of color to gain true equality within societies that were formerly riddled with internal colonialist mentalities, integration between classes and, particularly, racial and ethnic groups must be put into effect in full force. Former Justice of the Peace Bardwell's lack of belief in marrying an interracial couple manifests that integration is still problematic to some of those of the white race. This is a crucial issue because it will take cooperation from those of the white race in order to truly build equity among persons of color and Whites alike. Verily, it is imperative to understand that societal integration does not only occur through polity, economy and education; it can also be realized through family. Familial integration between various racial and ethnic groups very well might be just as beneficial of an aspect as political, economic, and educational integration in building a more equitable social structure as a whole.

Ultimately, white power has historically played an indelible role in the plight of the present-day condition of persons of color due to the historically bigoted ideals, racism, and prejudice that continues to drive the abject status of non-white people in the Western World. At its inception, the purpose of Eurocentrism was to, through contemptuous presumptions, hold other groups in humiliating inferiority, and celebrate their own Western European culture in honorific superiority. In relating to today's context, Eurocentric notions have adversely impacted the psychological mentality of individuals of minority groups. It is by no coincidence that favorableness and preference is implicitly associated to the white race even amongst young black children.

This was even the case during Kenneth (1914-2005) and Mamie Clark's (1917-1983) "doll experiments" taken on young African-American children in segregated schools during the middle twentieth century. In this study, two dolls—one brown-skinned and one fair-skinned—were presented in front of these minority children. The dolls were identical with the exception of skin complexion and hair color; however, the results showed that the fair-skinned white doll was unanimously favored among those children even though these children generally resembled the brown-skinned African-American doll in appearance. It is by no question a resulting factor of Eurocentric values imposed upon western societies that compelled and continue to compel minority children to attribute positive qualities to Euro-based aspects and negative qualities to Afro-based ones. The underlying problem within all of this is that these individuals themselves are African-descended individuals.

By my estimation, the remedy for the elimination of Eurocentric-based inequality is through integration—for it is common knowledge that "race," in itself, is merely a social construct. And, as thoroughly introduced, the concept of race emerged as a socio-political construct that was designed in an effort to bar certain individuals, by virtue of the social actions and the agendas of those who ran the world, of the rights, privileges, and *modes de vie* that certain groups in particular enjoyed in overwhelmingly disproportionate excesses. Therefore, integration of race by default implies the integration of social classes; and an integrated society whereby Blacks and Whites are looked upon as equals is the only way in which white racism and racial supremacy can be truly eradicated. If this measure is truly effectuated, then there might very well be a veritable "post-racial America" for the fruitful wellbeing of future generations to come.

Verily, a postmodern society free of "race" and racism is something that overshadows the legacy of the postbellum mulatto. In many more ways than one, the mulatto of the Postbellum South was striving to work through the socio-political issues pitted against him by looking to his partial European heritage in an effort to gain more respectable civic standing alongside Whites. In self-segregating himself from the black masses during this era, he was also doing away with the very asset that would later empower him—his kinship to the masses of black people that would later assist him in bringing about the change that he wished to see in the world. The people, custom, and class comprising the mulattoes of the Postbellum South faded away throughout the annals of history because of its lack of concurrent relevance in bringing about advancement for persons of color in the context of contemporary society. However, the legacy of the postbellum mulattoes in the South remains that their audible voice in antiquity transfers as an opaque remnant in modernity—but the true visibility of the postbellum mulatto effectively lives on through the present-day equalities afforded to minority individuals because of precedent blazed forth by the mulatto of the Postbellum South.

Carlton Dubois McClain – A Comprehensive Overview

Carlton Dubois McClain, A.B. (born April 28, 1992), who performs musically under the mononym, Céran, is an American singer-songwriter, multi-instrumentalist, management consultant, visual artist, urbanist, actor, published author, and polyglot. Born and raised in Kansas City, Missouri, he gained local and regional recognition in his childhood and adolescence in classical music with accolades such as the Early Bach Award, the Paderewski Gold Medal, and a bronze medal-finish in the 2008 State of Kansas Piano Auditions. Upon earning his high school diploma as a National College Board Advanced Placement Scholar from the locally-renowned Pembroke Hill School in 2010, he was subsequently offered admission into the University of Tulsa School of Music, the University of Evansville Department of Music, the American Musical and Dramatic Academy, as well as the University of Missouri – Kansas City. After opting to enroll into the latter academic institution, he went on to graduate with the "cum laude" collegiate medallion in 2014 upon completing his undergraduate degree in Urban Studies with a concentration in Community Development and Housing alongside a minor in French language.

Leveraging his Bachelor of Arts degree in 2015, he successfully furthered his education by earning all 19.5 credit hours attempted as a candidate for a Master of Arts in Management from Wake Forest University School of Business, which eventually landed him full-time employment as a founding member and chairperson of an economic and business development organization, entitled, "Occupy Until He Comes Ministry Services, LLC," that he established in 2016 with his parents, the Rev. Coleman Douglas McClain, Sr., M.Div., MBA and Mrs. Evalin Élaine McClain (née Clariette), M.S., MPA. Ultimately, both of his parents' lineages trace to mulatto-identified persons originating paternally in Alabama and Virginia, and maternally in Louisiana and

Mississippi, respectively, prior to the Racial Integrity Laws of 1924 – 1930. Aside from his many successes in academia and his professional career, he is also a noted polyglot with proficiency in French, Spanish, and German, in addition to his native English and Louisiana Creole; these linguistic skills have also been recognized by various institutions—including the American Association of Teachers of French as well as the National College Board, with the former awarding him on three consecutive occasions (2008, 2009, 2010) as a National Laureate in the National French Contest culminating in a first-place regional finish and a sixth-place national finish in the contest in the final year.

In May of 2009, his acting expertise landed him induction into the International Thespian Society in recognition of his contributions to the Theatre, while his skills in visual art were commended four years prior with the Scholastic Art and Writing Award. He then went on to make his mark on both a national and international scale with the release of four commercially- and critically-acclaimed studio albums under the moniker, Céran—"The Art of Céran" (2012), "Verity" (2014), "Live, and Let Love" (2015), and "Holding Out Hope" (2017). He also gained national media attention in 2014 for publishing his first book, titled, "Mulattoes in the Postbellum South and Beyond," as a twenty-one-year-old that has since sold 100+ copies in the United States alone; shortly thereafter, he was cordially invited by renowned radio host, Joe Madison, to speak on Madison's award-winning, self-titled nationally-syndicated show on SiriusXM Radio the following summer. In all, his work in music has earned him 1,000+ streams and sales in 40+ countries globally and in all six of the habitable continents of the world, universal acclaim from entertainment critics including Alex Henderson (Billboard, All Music Guide), and has garnered him the distinction of living up to and surpassing the meaning and origin of his namesake, Céran—"the thunderer." Outside of his accomplishments in literature and the arts, he is also extensively involved in service to his community with over seventy-five hours of community service completed as of 2014, in addition to serving as the Youth Council President of the Johnson County, Kansas branch of the National Association for the Advancement of Colored People (NAACP) for two consecutive terms (2007-2008; 2008-2009).

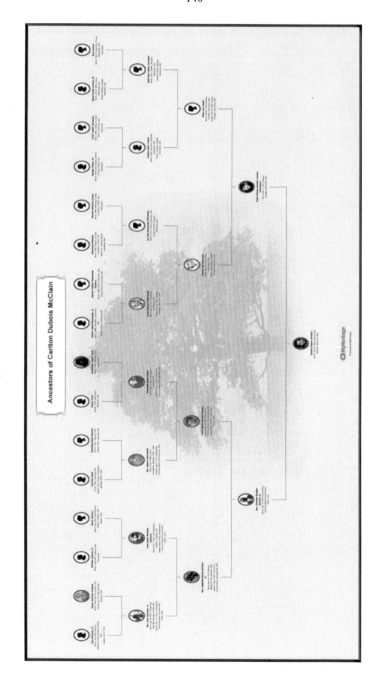

Ancestors of Carlton Dubois McClain

Carlton Dubois McClain's direct descent from William the Conqueror – King of England

I. William the Conqueror – King of England, married Matilda (daughter of Baldwin IV, Count of Flanders), and had:

II. Princess Gundred, married William, Earl of Warren, in Normandy, and had:

III. William de Warren, (2nd Earl of Warren and Surrey), married Lady Isabel of Vermandois (daughter of Hubert, 4th Count of Vermandois, by Lady Alice, his wife, daughter of Hugh the Great, Count of Vermandois, son of **Henry I – King of France**, by Anne of Kiev, his wife, daughter of **Yaroslav the Wise – Grand Prince of Kievan Rus'** by his wife Princess Ingegerd Olofsdotter of Sweden), and had:

IV. Lady Ada de Warren, married Prince Henry of Scotland (son of **David I – King of the Scots**, by Lady Matilda, his wife, daughter of Waltheof, Earl of Northumberland), and had:

V. Princess Marjory (sister of **King Malcolm IV** and **King William the Lion (William I of Scotland)**), married Gilchrist, Earl of Angus, and had:

VI. Lady Beatrix, married Walter Stuart, the 5th Lord High Steward and Justiciary of Scotland, and had:

VII. Lady Margaret Stuart, married Calin Fitzgerald, 1st Lord of Kentail, and had:

VIII. Kenneth, 2nd Lord of Kentail, married Lady Morba Macdonald, daughter of Alexander, Lord of Lorn, and had:

IX. Kenneth MacKenneth, 3rd Lord of Kentail, married Lady Margaret, daughter of David de Strathbogie, Earl of Athol, and had:

X. Kenneth MacKenzie, 4th Lord of Kentail, married Lady Fynvola, daughter of Roderick Macleod, of Lewes, and had:

XI. Murdock MacKenzie—Don, 5th Lord of Kentail, married Lady Isabel, daughter of Murdoch Macaula, of Lochbroom, and had:

XII. Murdoch MacKenzie, 6th Lord of Kentail, married Lady Fynvola, daughter of Macleod, of Harris, and had:

XIII. Alexander MacKenzie, 7th Lord of Kentail, married Lady Agnes Campbell, daughter of Colin, 1st Lord of Argyle, and had:

XIV. Sir Kenneth MacKenzie, 8th Lord of Kentail, married Lady Agnes, daughter of Hugh, Lord of Lovat, and had:

XV. John MacKenzie, 9th Lord of Kentail, married Elizabeth Grant, and had:

XVI. Kenneth MacKenzie, 10th Lord of Kentail, married Lady Elizabeth Stuart, daughter of John, Earl of Atholl, and had:

XVII. Lady Agnes MacKenzie, married **Lachlan Mohr MacIntosh, 16th Chief of Clan Chattan**, and had:

XVIII. William MacIntosh (of Essick and Borlum), married Elizabeth MacIntosh (née Innes), and had:

XIX. Lachlan MacIntosh (2nd proprietor of Borlum), married Lady Annie, and had:

XX. William MacIntosh, married Mary MacIntosh (née Baillie), and had:

XXI. Lachlan MacIntosh (of Knocknagail), married Mary MacIntosh (née Lockhart), and had:

XXII. John Mohr MacIntosh (1700 – 1761), married Marjory MacIntosh (née Frazer), and had:

XXIII. John McIntosh (27 April 1728 – 12 November 1826), married Margaret McIntosh (née McGillivray) (sister of wealthy Scots planter and fur trader, Lachlan McGillivray), and had:

XXIV. Captain William McIntosh, Sr. (1745 – *Deceased*) (brother-in-law of George Troup, by his wife, Catherine McIntosh, mother of

George McIntosh Troup, 32nd Governor of Georgia), married *Senoya Henneha*, (1758 – 1779), and had:

XXV. Creek Chief William H. McIntosh *Taskanugi Hatke* (White Warrior) (1775 – 1825), married Elizabeth "Eliza" McIntosh (née Grierson) (1780 – 1856) (daughter of wealthy Scots fur trader Robert Grierson and his wife, a high-status Shawnee woman, *Sinnugee*), and had:

XXVI. Chillicothe "Chilly" McIntosh (1795 – 1879), married Katie Casey McIntosh (née Hale) (1795 – *Deceased*), and had:

XXVII. Josiah Joseph McIntosh (1811 – 1921), married Rachel McIntosh (1830 – 1879), and had:

XVIII. George McIntosh (1854 – 1916), married Ella McIntosh (née Fobbs) (1854 – 1934), and had:

XXIX. Florance "Flora" McIntosh (1882 – 1909), was the wife of:

XXX. George S. Rambo (1877 – 1963), was, by way of the aforestated Florance "Flora" McIntosh (1882 – 1909), the father of:

XXXI. Eurleyne Lynette Rambo Levison (1929 – 2010), was the wife of:

XXXII. Simon Curtis Levison, Jr. (1913 – 2009), was, by way of Simon Levison, Sr. (1880 – *Deceased*) and his wife, Eva Levison (1880 – *Deceased*), the elder brother of:

XXXIII. Ruth Ann Levison (1921 – *Deceased*), courted Charles Mack Yarber (1920 – *Deceased*), and had:

XXXIV. Mary Lou Yarber (1940 – 1997), courted Alonzo Lee Patterson (1937 – 2011), and had:

XXXV. Evalin Élaine McClain (née Yarber (Clariette)) (1957 – Present), married Coleman Douglas McClain, Sr. (1955 – Present), and had:

XXXVI. Carlton Dubois McClain (28 April 1992 – Present)

Creek-Scots Chief, William H. McIntosh *Taskanugi Hatke* (White Warrior), is the great-great-grandfather of the wife of the father of the sister-in-law of Carlton's great-grandmother.

Bibliography

Aspen Institute Roundtable. *Structural Racism and Community Building.* Washington, D. C.: Aspen Institute Roundtable on Community Change, 2004.

Browning, Charles Henry. *Americans of Royal Descent: Collection of Genealogies Showing the Lineal Descent from Kings of Some American Families ...* Reprinted for Clearfield Co. by Genealogical Pub. Co., 2000.

"Census Records." *Census Records.* National Archives. Web. 08 Jan. 2014.

Cherry, Robert. "The Culture-of-Poverty Thesis and African Americans: The Work of Gunnar Myrdal and Other Institutionalists." *Journal of Economic Issues* 29.4 (1995): 1119-1131. Print.

Chestnutt, Charles W. "The Wife of His Youth." *The Atlantic.* The Atlantic, 1 July 1898. Web. 15 Jan. 2014.

"Chevalier de Saint-George - Griot Pictures." *Chevalier de Saint-George.* Griot Entertainment, LLC. Web. 08 Jan. 2014.

Church, Randolph W. and Waverly K. Winfree. *The Laws of Virginia: Being a Supplement to Hening's The Statutes at Large, 1700-1750.* Richmond: Virginia State Library, 1971.

Cox, Oliver C. *Caste, Class, & Race: A Study in Social Dynamics.* New York: Monthly Review, 1959.

"Criminal Justice Fact Sheet." *NAACP.* National Association for the Advancement of Colored People. Web. 07 Jan. 2014.

Davis, Floyd James. *Who Is Black?: One Nation's Definition.* University Park, PA: Pennsylvania State UP, 1991.

Douglass, Frederick. *Narrative of the Life of Frederick Douglass.* New York: Dover Publications, 1995.

Du Bois, W. E. B. and David L. Lewis. *Black Reconstruction in America.* New York: Simon & Schuster, 1995.

Du Bois, W. E. B., and Isabel Eaton. *The Philadelphia Negro.* New York, NY: Cosimo, 2007.

East, Don C. *A Historical Analysis of the Creek Indian Hillabee Towns: and Personal Reflections on the Landscape and People of Clay County Alabama.* IUniverse, 2008

Ellzey, Don. "JP Refuses to Marry Couple." *Hammond Star.* Hammond Star, 15 Oct. 2009. Web. 17 Jan. 2014.

Guillory, Monique. "Under One Roof: The Sins and Sanctity of the New Orleans Quadroon Balls." Race Consciousness. New York University Press, 1997.

Hochschild, Jennifer L. and Brenna M. Powell. "Racial Reorganization and the United States Census 1850-1930: Mulattoes, Half-Breeds, Mixed Parentage, Hindoos, and the Mexican Race." *Studies in American Political Development.* 2008; 22 (1): 59-96.

Hudson-Weems, Clenora. "Africana Womanism and the Critical Need for Africana Theory and Thought." *The Western Journal of Black Studies* 21.2 (1997): 79-84.

Janos, Andrew C. *East Central Europe in the Modern World: The Politics of the Borderlands from Pre- to Postcommunism.* Stanford, CA: Stanford UP, 2000.

Khanna, Nikki. *Biracial in America: Forming and Performing Racial Identity.* Lanham, MD: Lexington, 2011.

Lewis, Oscar. *Five Families: Mexican Case Studies in the Culture of Poverty.* New York: New American Library, 1959.

Marx, Karl. *Das Kapital: Kritik Der Politischen Ökonomie.* Berlin: Dietz, 1956.

Massey, Douglas S., and Nancy A. Denton. *American Apartheid: Segregation and the Making of the Underclass.* Harvard University Press, 2003.

McClain, Reginald D. *From Pillar to Post: Nobody Told Me My Way Would Be Easy.* Columbus, GA: Brentwood Christian, 2003.

McClain, Reginald D. Personal Interview. 26 Apr. 2009.

Miller, James. *American Slavery.* San Diego, California: Greenhaven Press, Inc., 2001.

Muhlenfeld, Elisabeth and C. Vann Woodward, eds., *The Private Mary Chesnut: The Unpublished Civil War Diaries* [New York and Oxford: Oxford University Press, 1984], pp. 30-33.

Myrdal, Gunnar. *An American Dilemma: The Negro Problem and Modern Democracy*. New York: Harper & Row, 1962.

"Obama Checks 'Black,' Gets Side Eye from Some." *The Root*. Web. 08 Jan. 2014.

Patrick-Wexler, Diane. *The New York Public Library Amazing African American History*. New York: Wiley, 1998.

Popkin, Jeremy. "H-France Review Vol. 4." *H-France Reviews*. September 2004. The Society for French Historical Studies. 10 Jan. 2014.

Rodney, Walter. *How Europe Underdeveloped Africa*. Washington, D.C.: Howard University Press, 1981.

Russell-Cole, Kathy, Midge Wilson, and Ronald E. Hall. *The Color Complex: The Politics of Skin Color in a New Millennium*. New York: Anchor, 2013.

Sailer, Steve. "Race Now: #2: How White Are Blacks? How Black Are Whites?"*Mark. D. Shriver, Admixture, Genetic, Gene, Race, Miscegenation, African-American, Passing, Sally Hemings*. United Press International, Inc. Web. 08 Jan. 2014.

Smith, Adam. *An Inquiry into the Nature and Causes of the Wealth of Nations*. New York: Modern Library, 1937.

South Carolina Government of 1860. *Declaration of the Immediate Causes Which Induce and Justify the Secession of South Carolina from the Federal Union and the Ordinance of Secession.* Charleston: Evans & Cogswell, Printers to the Convention, 1860.

West, Cornel. *Toward a Socialist Theory of Racism*. New York, NY: Institute for Democratic Socialism, 1989.

White, Walter F. *A Man Called White: The Autobiography of Walter White.* Athens: University of Georgia, 1995.

Williamson, Jeffrey G., and Peter H. Lindert. *American Inequality: A Macroeconomic History*. New York: Academic, 1980.

Zinn, Howard. *A People's History of the United States: 1492-present.* New York: Harper Collins, 2003.

Made in the USA
Columbia, SC
11 March 2019